Protecting Markets

Also by the author

Hawke's Law: The Politics of Mining and Aboriginal Land Rights in Australia

The Politics of Economic Power in Southern Africa

Toward an Africanized U.S. Policy for Southern Africa

PROTECTING MARKETS

U.S. Policy and the
World Grain Trade

Ronald T. Libby

Cornell University Press

Ithaca and London

Copyright © 1992 by Cornell University

All rights reserved. Except for brief quotations in a review,
this book, or parts thereof, must not be reproduced in any
form without permission in writing from the publisher.
For information, address Cornell University Press,
124 Roberts Place, Ithaca, New York 14850.

First published 1992 by Cornell University Press.

International Standard Book Number 0-8014-2617-0
Library of Congress Catalog Card Number 91-55536
Printed in the United States of America
Librarians: Library of Congress cataloging information
appears on the last page of the book.

⊚ The paper in this book meets the minimum
requirements of the American National Standard for
Information Sciences—Permanence of Paper for
Printed Library Materials. ANSI Z39.48-1984.

IN MEMORY OF
H. B. "BARNEY" JACOBSON
AND GALVA, IOWA

Contents

Contents

[*viii*]

Figures and Tables

Figures

Tables

Preface

Commentators acknowledge that mercantilism is a major approach to understanding international political economy. Robert Gilpin (1975), for example, notes three prevailing conceptions of political economy: liberalism, Marxism, and mercantilism. Mercantilism is associated with the subservience of the economy to the state and its interests, which range from national security to domestic economic welfare. Charles Kindleberger observes that challenging powers in world politics use mercantilist policies, whereas challenged powers try to perpetuate universal free trade. Yet he points out that the United Kingdom and the United States have not consistently followed free trade policies during the nineteenth and twentieth centuries (private communication, November 12, 1990; Kindleberger, 1978). Indeed, Jagdish Bhagwati and Douglas Irwin (1987) argue that mercantilism rather than free trade has been the rule in American trade policy.

Despite these acknowledgments, there are virtually no contemporary studies of U.S. mercantilist trade policies—perhaps because political economists are trained in the neoclassical tradition. T. K. Warley (1976:292–93) points out, however, that classical trade theory is at such variance with reality that it fails to provide an adequate basis for explaining international trade.

Unquestionably, classical trade theory is frustrated by international trade. The chasm between theory and reality has never been greater, and we need alternative approaches to international trade.

This book analyzes what I believe is a contemporary instance of U.S. mercantilism in trade policy—an aggressive retaliatory agricultural policy called the Export Enhancement Program. To my knowledge there are no other contemporary studies of mercantilism, so this book is a pioneering effort. There is no theoretical literature or, indeed, mercantilist cases within which to situate my work. Nevertheless, I hope this book will stimulate further studies of mercantilism.

The idea for the book originated during the 1985–86 academic year, while I was a visiting professor in the Department of Political Science at Northwestern University. My earlier research on Africa had forced me to consider global problems of the production and distribution of food. It was difficult for me to reconcile the widespread shortages of food in Africa and the Caribbean with the mountains of surplus food in the United States and Western Europe.

My visit to Northwestern gave me the opportunity to satisfy my curiosity about the world grain trade, since the Chicago Board of Trade (CBT) was close by. The CBT is one of the chief trading centers for the world grain trade—it determines world prices. I decided to teach a seminar on the politics of world food, at which several grain analysts generously agreed to speak.

During one session Dale Gustafson, a grain analyst with Drexel, Burnham, Lambert, Inc., offered an intriguing proposition: the United States could apply political pressure on the European Community's budget by subsidizing the export of surplus U.S. grain. With continuing large inventories of world grain and low world prices, the EC would be forced to increase subsidies in order to export its surplus grain. Furthermore, if the U.S. dollar dropped from its 1985 peak, the European Community would immediately experience great financial pressure to increase its export subsidies beyond its budgetary resources.

The U.S. policy that sought to apply this political pressure on the EC was the Export Enhancement Program, which became operational in September 1985. From that date until the end of 1990, I carefully tracked the program and reactions to it. I collected weekly announcements by the U.S. Department of Agriculture and weekly reports on the EC grain trade issued by the Home-Grown Cereals Authority of London. E. M. Low, head of marketing and economics of the Home-Grown Cereals Authority of London, kindly provided the EC data for Tables 4.2 and 4.3. Thomas O. Kay, the administrator of the USDA Foreign Agricultural Service; Melvin E. Simms, the general sales manager and vice-president of the Commodity Credit Corporation; L. T. McElvain, the acting director of the Commodity Credit Corporation's Operations Division Export Credits; and William S. Hawkins, the agricultural marketing specialist in the Foreign Agricultural Service, were also helpful in providing data for Tables 4.2 and 4.3 and other material on the Export Enhancement Program.

The Treasury and Parliamentary libraries of the New Zealand government also provided access to their holdings on the European Community. Officials of the U.S. Department of Agriculture; the U.S. Senate Committee on Agriculture, Nutrition, and Forestry; and the U.S. General Accounting Office also gave their time and advice, as did officials of the Australian Bureau of Agricultural and Resource Economics in Canberra and the Directorate-General for Agriculture of the Commission of the European Communities. The Center for Rural Affairs of Walthill, Nebraska, gave me access to their informative reports on U.S. farm policy. The Home-Grown Cereals Authority of London provided published and unpublished documents on European grain production and exports. The office of Senator Kent Conrad (N.D.) provided invaluable information on Congress, and Cargill, Inc., made available its file of information on the Export Enhancement Program. Peter Lilley, the financial secretary to the British Treasury, also assisted in the research.

I express my appreciation to these and other institutions and individuals who contributed to this book. The Internal Research Committee of Victoria University of Wellington, New Zealand, where I was a faculty member from 1987 to 1989, provided funds for research assistance in the early stages. Dina Nieuweveen, my research assistant, compiled most of the data for the project. Her meticulous attention to detail forced me to reconcile seemingly inexplicable differences in data. She is largely responsible for the accuracy of the tables and figures in Chapter 4. Robin Mita was responsible for most of the diagrams and figures; Mary Alice Matthews designed Figure 2.3; Victoria Halfmann prepared Figure 3.2; and Charles Myrbach designed Figures 2.2 and 6.1.

Susan Strange of the European University Institute read and commented on a first draft of the book manuscript. C. Ford Runge of the University of Minnesota; Professor Dr. E.-O. Czempiel of the Johann Wolfgang Goethe-Universität, Frankfurt on the Main; Ivan Roberts of the Australian Bureau of Agricultural and Resource Economics; and Jean-Baptiste Danel, agricultural counselor to the Embassy of France in the United States, also read and commented on the entire manuscript. Donald Puchala and Alan Cafruny, the readers for Cornell University Press, provided penetrating and informative criticism of the work.

Jerry Sharples and James Vertrees of the Economic Research Service of the U.S. Department of Agriculture read and commented on draft sections, as did Robert Paarlberg, Dan McGuire (formerly director of the Nebraska Wheat Board), and Lynnett Wagner, a staff member of the U.S. Senate Committee on Agriculture. For comments on theoretical sections of the book I thank Stephen Krasner, Peter Katzenstein, Charles Kindleberger, John Zysman, Robert Kudrle, Miles Kahler, and Paul Krugman.

I express my appreciation for assistance at the final stages of the book to Southwest State University's Vice-President for Academic Affairs, Ned Conway. SSU's representative on the Minnesota State University Board, Julie Bleyhl, kindly arranged comments from representatives of U.S. farm organizations. Arlene Schoephoerster, supervisor of the university's word-processing center, was indispensable in preparing the final manuscript. My editor at Cornell University Press, Roger Haydon, encouraged me at difficult phases of the work and shepherded the manuscript to publication. Janet Mais did an excellent job editing the manuscript.

My greatest debt of gratitude is to my wife, Kathleen Christina, and my daughter, Kathleen Elizabeth. They consistently supported me through long and difficult periods of research, writing, and rewriting. They believed in the value of my work even when I had doubts.

RONALD T. LIBBY

Marshall, Minnesota

Abbreviations

CAP	Common Agricultural Policy
CCC	Commodity Credit Corporation
COGECA	Comité Général de la Coopération Agricole des Pays de la CEE (General Committee of Agricultural Cooperation in the EC)
COPA	Comité des Organisations Professionnelles Agricoles de la Communauté Européenne (Committee of Agricultural Organizations in the European Community)
EAGGF	European Agricultural Guidance and Guarantee Fund
EC	European Community
ECU	European currency unit
EEP	Export Enhancement Program
FAS	Foreign Agricultural Service
GATT	General Agreement on Tariffs and Trade
HGCA	Home-Grown Cereals Authority
MCA	monetary compensatory amount
MGQ	maximum guaranteed quantity
OMB	Office of Management and Budget
SGCI	Secrétariat Général du Comité Interministériel pour les Questions Européennes
USDA	U.S. Department of Agriculture
VAT	value-added tax

Protecting Markets

Introduction

This book evaluates the effectiveness of a recent American experiment with mercantilism in trade policy, the Export Enhancement Program (EEP). Adopted during the second Reagan administration in 1985 in retaliation against the European Community's program of subsidizing agricultural exports, the EEP was meant to increase the financial burden of the EC's Common Agricultural Policy (CAP) to a politically unacceptable level. The plan was to exacerbate political tensions within the EC, especially between Great Britain and France. The British resented the large and growing burden of financing agricultural exports primarily for France's benefit. If the EC could be persuaded to reduce its budgetary support for agricultural exports, the United States might be able indirectly to pressure the French government into negotiating reductions in agricultural export subsidies in the context of the General Agreement on Tariffs and Trade (GATT). The Americans reasoned that without the EC's high export subsidies, the French could not retain the markets they had taken from the United States. The United States would reestablish its dominance of the world grain trade and thus improve its deteriorating balance of payments.

The Uruguay Round of GATT Negotiations

The significance of the EEP lies in the U.S. strategy for the eighth round of GATT talks launched in Punta del Este, Uruguay, in 1986 and lasting until the end of 1991. To understand the American trade strategy, some background is necessary. The talks were initiated primarily at the insistence of the United States in response to the fragmentation of the world economy into rival trading blocs drifting steadily apart. Western Europe and Japan had become major industrial powers, and the winding down of the Cold War was fostering the further development of trading blocs.

In 1989 the United States–Canada Free Trade Agreement came into force, substantially increasing cross-border trade by eliminating most tariffs and removing financial restrictions on service industries, such as banks and insurance companies, operating in both countries. A similar bilateral trade agreement between the United States and Mexico, which could follow as early as 1993, would remove U.S. trade barriers against Mexican imports, increase the U.S. labor market by some 60 million people, and increase Mexican oil production with high-technology U.S. drilling and exploration equipment. The European Community has accused the Americans of sealing off North American markets and thereby strangling free trade.

But the EC has itself embarked on a process of strengthening the community as an economic bloc, to counter U.S. and Japanese economic and industrial power. The Single European Act was first proposed in 1985 but formally adopted in 1987. Its purpose is to establish a barrier-free internal market of 320 million people in twelve European countries. The EC has made it clear that foreign-based corporations will be denied the status and privileges of European firms, unless specifically provided for by reciprocal agreements with foreign governments.

The United States has responded to the Single European Act with foreboding because it expects the Europeans to erect barriers to the single internal market in 1993. European governments may well be pressured to compensate European producers for increased domestic competition within the EC by controlling competitive pressure from outside. Peter McPherson, U.S. deputy treasury secretary, has warned that the creation of a market preserving Europe for the Europeans would be bad for both Europe and the United States, while others have criticized the Single European Act for fostering European protectionism and discrimination against American imports (*German Tribune*, September 4, 1988:3).

World trade has increased every year since World War II. From 1958 to 1990, it grew at a faster rate than worldwide gross national product. From 1958 to 1978, trade increased fivefold, and during the 1980s it almost doubled, but with much of the increase occurring within trading blocs. While ideas, goods, services, and capital have moved more freely, worldwide multilateral exchange has increasingly been supplanted by bilateral exchange through government agreements. The EC has agreed with the Japanese on how many cars Japan may ship to Europe, and the United States has negotiated with the Europeans the share of the U.S. steel market European producers can obtain. The major trading blocs (the United States, the EC, and Japan) seem more and more to resort to a managed system of international trade, leaving the smaller states at a disadvantage. But managed trade, by shielding markets from foreign competition, makes goods and services too expensive and protects outmoded and inefficient national producers.

It was in this context that the Reagan administration pressed for a new round of GATT talks, hoping to remove the barriers to U.S. exporters which rival trading blocs were erecting. Intense American lobbying brought agreement on a fifteen-point program for GATT negotiations which stated that trade must be based on fair competition and that agricultural trading must be based on fairer rules that do not hamper efficient producers. Although the Uruguay round's negotiating agenda included fifteen trade topics ranging from open borders for telecommunications, television, finance, credit, and insurance to protection of intellectual property such as patents, agricultural trade was the chief U.S. concern. Sharing in this concern were many Third World countries and the fourteen major exporters of agricultural produce who make up the Cairns Group (named after an Austra-

[3]

lian town). Together they made success in agricultural trade policy a precondition for success in eliminating protectionist policies in other areas.

Indeed, the principal dispute in the Uruguay round was between the United States and the European Community over agricultural trade policy, and behind that dispute was a long history of U.S.-EC conflict. During the Kennedy round of GATT negotiations from 1962 to 1967, the United States pressured the Europeans to allow the unhindered export of cheap corn-gluten feed into the European Community. That episode, among other considerations, left the EC unenthusiastic about the Tokyo round of GATT negotiations between 1973 and 1979, where the community would again come under U.S. pressure to alter its highly protectionist agricultural policies.

The Uruguay round meant more of the same, only this time the United States demanded the return of agricultural markets it had lost to the European community. The U.S. position was that these agricultural markets were lost because of European export subsidies averaging $5 billion annually. In reality, subsidies were at the heart of the agricultural trade debate. Recent government farm spending worldwide had averaged between $200 billion and $300 billion annually. The EC alone is responsible for more than $90 billion of that spending, with the United States accounting for about $70 billion and Third World countries roughly $60 billion. The Americans were particularly irate because they viewed the United States as the world's most efficient producer and traditionally Europe's major supplier of food imports. They insisted that the same rules that apply to trade in manufactured goods must also apply to agriculture. This demand led to an impasse because the EC recognized that European farmers could not compete unsubsidized in world markets. The large farms in the U.S. Midwest produce food grain at lower cost than family farms in France or southwest Germany, and the cost of producing beef in Argentina is far lower than the cost in the European Community.

During the latter stages of the Uruguay round, the U.S. delegation modified its demand that the EC abolish its farm subsidies within ten years and insisted instead that the community reduce its overall farm support by 75 percent and its export sub-sidies by 90 percent over the ten years. The EC rejected the U.S. demand and offered a modest 30 percent cut in farm support over ten years. But there was a catch: because the EC proposal was retroactive to 1986 and would therefore include the cuts imposed that year, it really called for a cut of only 15 percent or less over the next five years. In making this counterproposal, the EC was painfully aware that without high levels of export sub-sidies members could not sell their farm produce outside the community, which would lead to a decline in agricultural out-put and force many of its 11 million farmers to give up their farms. So the Europeans argued that agricultural policy was a minor trade issue, with farm exports constituting less than 10 percent of U.S. and EC exports, and that the United States was equally guilty of protectionist practices such as providing gen-erous farm subsidies and adopting discriminatory trade legisla-tion in the guise of the U.S. Trade Act. That act, signed by President George Bush in 1988, created a statutory obligation to enact punitive import bans and tariffs against countries Con-gress deemed guilty of "unfair" trade practices.

Just before the breakdown of the Uruguay round in December 1990, U.S. agriculture secretary Clayton Yeutter said that if the EC did not agree to reform its agriculture policy, the United States was prepared to "bankrupt the European Community with a trade war" (*Agweek*, December 24, 1990:42), and Carla Hills, the U.S. trade representative, said that the United States refused to budge on its demand that the EC reform its agricul-tural policies and that agricultural export subsidies remained the "crux of the matter" (*German Tribune*, June 17, 1990:7).[1]

The United States had the means to finance a trade war under the GATT contingency clause of the October 1990 deficit reduc-tion bill, which authorized the Treasury to finance such a war.

---

[1] The initial round of the Uruguay GATT trade talks broke down primarily over the European Community's refusal to accept U.S. demands for deep cuts in export subsidies. The talks were revived in May 1991 in Geneva and were scheduled to end in December 1991. The French have been the most determined opponents of any attempt to reform the EC's agricultural subsidy policies (*Ag-week*, May 6, 1991:15).

The clause, which restored approximately $5 billion of the $13.6 billion in subsidies cut from the 1990 farm bill (covering a five-year period), was added to the deficit reduction bill after intense negotiations between Congress and the White House. It would enable the United States to increase grain export subsidies by $1 billion under the Export Enhancement Program. In March 1991, Congress approved a "dire emergency" spending bill that gave the USDA unlimited spending authority to support the EEP in response to competition from the EC (*Agweek*, March 25, 1991: 10). Although the EEP is one of the principal U.S. trade weapons for countering European farm export subsidies, there is controversy over its effectiveness and the wisdom of using it. Critics argue that the program is costly and wasteful and too small anyway to have a real impact. Furthermore, they point out, a bigger effort might only trigger an agricultural trade war with the European Community, which could damage the economies of major agricultural exporting countries that do not subsidize farm exports.

Proponents of the EEP argue, however, that given the large agricultural output of the United States and its resources, the program could place a significant financial burden on the EC. They reason that the European Community cannot incur a budget deficit without the agreement of all twelve member states. Given the history of intracommunity quarrels over the size and burden sharing of contributions to the EC budget, an agricultural subsidy war could tip the balance toward members favoring reduced agricultural subsidies and lead ultimately to their elimination. A brief examination of the arguments for and against the Export Enhancement Program illustrates the nature of the controversy.

The Cases against and for the U.S. Strategy

The conventional wisdom holds that mercantilist trade policies such as the EEP are wasteful, self-defeating, and dangerous insofar as they tend to stimulate retaliation and trade warfare. Robert Paarlberg (1988:4), for example, argues that the use of export subsidies to dispose of surplus production in contracting world markets during the 1980s lowered world prices and dramatically increased the costs of farm programs. He points out that the U.S. farm budget increased from about $5 billion in the early 1980s to approximately $26 billion in 1986; over the same period, the cost of the European Community's farm programs and subsidies doubled to about $23 billion. He warns that in addition to the high cost of subsidies, there is the underlying danger of an agricultural trade war.

Paarlberg (1989) also discounts the Export Enhancement Program's value as an instrument of foreign policy. He argues that the EEP did not significantly increase the costs of subsidizing EC agricultural exports. The additional cost to the European Community, he claims, was only between $380 million and $430 million in 1987 and between $270 million and $320 million in 1988. (The Australian Bureau of Agricultural and Resource Economics has estimated the additional cost to the EC budget for wheat alone to be $400 million in 1987 and $300 million in 1988.) Paarlberg estimates that only 1 to 1.5 percent of the EC budgetary expenditure went for agricultural subsidies (1989:8), and he asserts that this "unfortunate export subsidy war" backfired, putting more pressure on the United States than on the European Community. The United States has the most to lose from a trade war, in this view; for it is the largest agricultural exporter in the world, would have to spend the most to sustain the competition, and has the largest number of agricultural markets to forfeit.

Paarlberg rejects as well the argument that the Export Enhancement Program was an effective bargaining chip in the Uruguay round of GATT talks. The EEP had neither increased pressures on the CAP budget nor exacted significant costs in EC markets lost. Moreover, it was too small to help U.S. negotiators bargain for reductions in the European Community's export subsidies. Note, however, that Paarlberg's argument does not undercut mercantilist trade policies as such; in fact, it does the reverse. To be an effective foreign policy tool, the Export Enhancement Program would have to be large enough to persuade the EC to negotiate its subsidies. Paarlberg's argument actually calls for a larger subsidy program, not its elimination. Nevertheless, he claims that the EEP was big enough to divert international criticism from the EC's high subsidies; potential U.S. allies, particularly the Cairns Group and the Canadian government, criticized U.S. trade policy instead, weakening the U.S. bargaining position in the Uruguay round.

Paarlberg prescribes standard liberal economic policy to deal with trade competition from the EC: he argues for unilaterally dismantling U.S. farm support policies. For example, he proposes lowering target prices (federal goals for farm income) that "break the budget" and decoupling payments to farmers from production, two steps he regards as desirable whether or not the United States reaches agreement with the EC in GATT talks. His rationale is that these actions will lower world prices and thereby increase pressure on the budgets of foreign countries that subsidize exports (1988:135). Of course the danger of unilaterally dismantling U.S. farm supports, apart from the immediate and potentially devastating impact on American farmers, is the lack of any guarantee that the EC would dismantle its farm supports. In fact, the evidence suggests they would do just the opposite—increase agricultural production and try to take markets away from the United States. This is precisely the reason Senator Kent Conrad proposed a bill in the Congress which would authorize the use of the EEP as a weapon against the European Community, or any countries, that do not decrease wheat acreage when the United States does (*Agweek*, September 17, 1990:21).

A report by David Harvey (1986), a British agricultural economist, gives an entirely different assessment of the Export Enhancement Program. Harvey argues that if the EC continues to allow cereal production to increase and continues to export surplus production, it could face bankruptcy because of the U.S. policy of "retaliatory subsidization." He challenges Paarlberg's assessment that the United States has the most to lose from a subsidy war. On the contrary, he argues, regardless of pressures on public expenditure and on the budget deficit, the United States is big enough and wealthy enough to retaliate effectively against heavily subsidized competition from the European Community.

He believes that in any "food trade war" the United States on its own could "break" the EC budget by depressing the world price of cereals.

Harvey offers this assessment of the EC's predicament: The European Community has gone beyond agricultural self-sufficiency to surplus production and now faces the need to expand its exports. World production is high, whereas world demand is low, a situation that is unlikely to change. Demand for cereals in Europe is stagnant; the states of the former USSR are increasing their output and moving toward self-sufficiency; the newly industrializing countries are committed to achieving self-sufficiency; and the less developed countries do not have the financial resources to create new markets for grain.

The economic crisis confronting the former USSR and Eastern Europe since Harvey's 1986 report is unlikely to change the market demand for grain. The former Soviet states do not have the financial resources or credit to afford large-scale food imports. The U.S. Department of Agriculture estimates that the integration of East Germany, with its large farm sector, into a united Germany and thus into the EC will contribute an additional 5 million metric tons of grain to world markets within a few years (*Agweek*, October 15, 1990:8).

According to Harvey's thinking, only an immediate reduction in cereal output can save the EC from a mounting agricultural bill. The rising cost of the grain sector can be checked only through major reductions in the support price for grain. Harvey estimates that reductions in the range of 6–7 percent in real terms would be required annually simply to hold the output of cereals constant. To cut back on production, the support price would have to be reduced by an even larger margin. Neither alternative is politically feasible because of the many small-scale farmers in Europe. Politicians fear the reaction of these voters to any policy that reduces farm income. This situation makes the European Community vulnerable to subsidy retaliation by the United States.

My own opinion is that a mercantilist trade strategy is an effective instrument of foreign policy. Unlike proponents of liberal trade theory, I believe an aggressive policy of trade reciprocity can provide a powerful incentive for a trade rival to negotiate reductions in trade barriers. In the case of the Export Enhancement Program, a retaliatory subsidy policy increased the political tension in the European Community by applying pressure on the Common Agricultural Policy budget. Political tension over the burden of financing the CAP budget already existed between the British, on one hand, and the French and the Germans, on the other. All the United States had to do to gain political leverage was to increase the cost of subsidies in the CAP budget.

The effectiveness of the Export Enhancement Program cannot, however, be judged solely or even primarily by the absolute cost to the EC of counteracting the U.S. subsidy program. In this regard, the analyses of both Paarlberg and Harvey are incomplete. Paarlberg minimizes the significance of the EEP, concluding that the economic costs to the EC were negligible; Harvey exaggerates its significance, arguing the United States is capable of "bankrupting" the EC through its subsidy program. Both exaggerate because they do not consider the EC's political reaction to the program.

In the pages that follow, I discuss the philosophical and strategic dimensions of mercantilist trade policy, of which the Export Enhancement Program is but one recent example, and go on to analyze the political impact of the EEP on the European Community and the successes and dangers of such a policy.

Chapter One

A Mercantilist Approach
to U.S. Farm Trade Policy

Congress began work on the Food Security Act of 1985 in an America that seemed to have lost its competitiveness in world food markets. U.S. commodity prices were inflated as a result of the high loan rates in the 1981 farm bill. Trading practices of competitors, particularly the European Community, were widely perceived as unfair. In its trade policy declaration accompanying the Food Security Act (*Congressional Record*, 1985:H12288), Congress elaborated a set of objectives and strategies for U.S. agricultural trade policy. Point 4 of Section 1121(b) states that the United States should "counter aggressively unfair foreign trade practices using all available means." The means the act provided was the Export Enhancement Program.

In a 1986 report to the president and Congress, the U.S. National Commission on Agricultural Trade and Export Policy proposed that "as a first step, we should resolve ourselves to achieve the goal of recapturing the total world market share of U.S. agricultural exports by commodity, achieved during the last period of major recent growth of such exports" (1986:16). In other words, the commission advocated the restoration of U.S. dominance of world agricultural markets, and since the Uruguay round of GATT talks, restoration of lost markets has indeed been a major U.S. foreign policy goal, with the EEP as its primary instrument. There are at least two theoretical approaches to evaluating the policy and the program, the neoclassical liberal approach and the mercantilist one. The choice determines whether the policy and the program are judged to be legitimate.

Liberal Trade Policy

The liberal approach to trade does not accept the restoration of U.S. market shares as a legitimate objective for the Export Enhancement Program. Liberal political economists view espousing historical market shares as a policy objective as simply a subterfuge to avoid openly promoting vested interests at the expense of a country's common good. Tangermann (1985:85) observes that to understand the real, as opposed to the declared, goals of any agricultural policy, we must go beyond the stated objectives of governments; for real policy objectives are often implicit in the implementation of policies and the motivation of policy makers. Don Paarlberg (1984:9) states bluntly that there are two goals in all U.S. farm policies which never appear in legislation and are seldom expressed openly in public meetings: "to support agriculture in the manner [to] which it has become accustomed" and "to elect or re-elect certain persons to public office."

This tendency to dismiss or underplay national interest as a legitimate objective in farm policy leads liberal economists to focus instead on how a policy affects farmers' income. Thus they evaluate the EEP in terms of its impact on price levels for grain and on income support levels for U.S. farmers. As they see it, although the EEP has tended to increase the price of exported commodities, most of the economic benefits have gone to the large farmers and to agribusiness corporations, such as Cargill and Continental Grain, who could operate profitably with or without the program. This criticism applies equally, however, to most farm programs.

Some liberal economists have gone so far as to discount the significance of the program almost entirely. They argue that fluctuations in the U.S. share of world grain markets have been

[12]

largely due to changes in the U.S. dollar exchange rate. For example, the U.S. share of the world wheat market was 44.7 percent of the total in 1980–81; by 1985–86, the U.S. share had fallen to only 28.6 percent—a decline of 16.1 percent. This loss of market share these economists blame on an overvalued U.S. dollar and a high farm loan rate for wheat, which together made American grain exports uncompetitive in the currencies of export rivals. The irony of this explanation is that this un-competitiveness led to the very accumulation of grain stocks which made the Export Enhancement Program possible. In other words, U.S. mismanagement of budgetary and farm policy led to the creation of the EEP, which was ostensibly designed to elimi-nate distortions in international trade which *other* countries had created.

Indeed, the Australian Bureau of Agricultural and Resource Economics (1989b:77) has even suggested that the purpose of the Export Enhancement Program may be unrelated to the de-clared objective of restoring U.S. markets. It hypothesizes that the EEP's real purpose was to win public support for "destock-ing," or unloading at taxpayers' expense, the huge reserves of grain the United States had accumulated during the 1983–87 period. In this explanation, the interests of farmers and agribusi-ness coincided with the U.S. government's need to deal with its balance-of-payments and foreign debt problems. The result was the creation of a powerful political market for protection. The public's perception of the loss of U.S. competitiveness resulting from unfair policies of the European Community and Japan provided an ideal political climate for U.S. adoption of another expensive farm support policy to sell accumulated surplus pro-duction. The difficulty with this interpretation is that the pro-gram continued after the surplus wheat stock had been disposed of and was even maintained during the severe drought of 1988–89, when U.S. production was at a forty-year low and there was no surplus grain.

Liberal economists have advocated maximizing national wel-fare through the efficient use of a country's resources. In the traditional Ricardian and Heckscher-Ohlin-Samuelson models of comparative advantage, individual countries gain from specializing in the production of those goods they can produce at the lowest relative cost while they purchase from other countries the goods they could only produce at relatively higher costs. Economic resources differ from country to country; some countries are more naturally suited to growing particular crops or livestock. For example, even though it is possible to grow wheat in countries with such diverse land, climate, technology, and labor forces as Norway, the United States, and China, the comparative advantages in wheat production differ. Although Norway can grow wheat, its comparative advantage in agriculture lies in dairy farming. Even though Norwegians can grow wheat as well as American farmers, they are unlikely to do so because they can buy more wheat with the money from selling dairy products than they could raise on their valuable land in their hostile climate.

Some liberal economists have begun to recognize the theoretical weakness of the principle of comparative advantage. The specialization of labor implicit in comparative advantage rests on interdependence and political trust among trading states, whereas in actuality nation-states constitute security zones of protection. States use their economic resources (including land and labor) to produce essential items regardless of comparative advantage (M. Strange, 1989:12). Grains in the European Community and rice in Japan can be grown more cheaply elsewhere, but these governments do not want to be politically dependent on other states for the supply of these nutritionally important commodities. For health reasons the EC has banned the importation (as well as the local production) of beef raised with hormones. Comparative advantage inevitably yields to the sovereign right of nation-states to guarantee the welfare of their citizenry. Other policy goals states may rationally choose over efficiency include protecting the social welfare of rural communities, environmental protection, national security, and social justice. From this perspective, action taken to serve legitimate national interests cannot be dismissed as simply "protectionism."

Another difficulty with the principle of comparative advantage is that natural advantages may not be fixed in location or even tangible. The United States and Japan have a comparative advantage in computer technology largely because of their superior educational systems and the presence of qualified scientists and technicians in large numbers—conditions that could change or be created elsewhere. One reason the United States has a comparative advantage in agriculture is that infrastructure including highways, ports, railroads, and storage facilities is highly developed; yet without major new investment, infrastructure will age and deteriorate, U.S. comparative advantage in agriculture will begin to decline, and other countries will produce farm products more cheaply.[1]

Awareness of the inadequacy of the concept of comparative advantage in trade has led to modifications, for example, the introduction of the term *competitive advantage* (Dunmore, 1986), which incorporates those actions of government intended to transform a country's comparative disadvantage to an advantage. Governments can engage in "clean" or "dirty" political action to increase their competitive advantage. Clean competitive advantage might be gained by establishing new schools, improving transportation systems, and constructing irrigation systems. Dirty competitive advantage might derive from using export subsidies, disregarding patent rights in other countries, and deliberately manipulating currency value. The distinction between clean and dirty competitive advantage can be fuzzy, however, and may be a function of whether a government or its trading rival draws the distinction.

Despite the obvious weakness of the principle of comparative advantage, the proponents of trade liberalization, or "free marketers," rely on it to justify their policy recommendations. They typically argue that the prices of goods set by national markets (unfettered by government interference) should be the basis for

---

[1] It is difficult to compare international costs of production. The cost of land, for example, fluctuates with inflation, interest rates, transportation costs, demands for nonfarm use of land, and the profitability of farming. Comparisons for major traded crops are both rarely done and inconclusive. One attempt, by the Kansas City Federal Reserve Bank (Barkema and Drabenstott, 1988), concluded that Argentina produces corn, wheat, and soybeans at a lower cost than the United States.

allocating resources within society (Lipton, 1987). But markets cannot perform this vital function because of trade barriers imposed by governments. These barriers distort markets and thus prevent nations from specializing in the production of goods in which they have an advantage. Governmental policies—agricultural subsidies and protectionism—artificially inflate the price of farm commodities, stimulating surplus production in developed countries, especially the United States, the European Community, and Japan.

Critics of the policy of trade liberalization dismiss it on the grounds that free or liberal trade is no policy at all; for it is predicated on the assumption that markets perform according to narrowly defined conditions that do not exist. One important condition is that there be no economic concentration or distortion in the marketplace of buyers and sellers sufficient to affect the market price of commodities. In the case of cereals, a handful of large multinational grain corporations dominate the trade. These oligopolies compete among themselves for markets and profits and act to protect their collective power (D. Morgan, 1980). Indeed, the foremost proponents of trade liberalization are large private trading companies; agricultural lenders and suppliers; and farm organizations that serve the interests of large, wealthy farmers. Their profits are guaranteed by trading farm commodities and do not depend on guaranteed farm income and price supports. In addition, most agricultural exporting countries have state marketing boards that significantly affect commodity production and pricing decisions. Without government intervention in the marketplace, private monopolies would determine national domestic and international policies toward production, distribution, and prices of agricultural commodities, all of which have significant implications for national welfare and security. Trade barriers exist precisely because markets do not operate according to the classical liberal conception, and governments do intervene to protect socioeconomic welfare and national security.

Liberal economists persist, nevertheless, in advocating the blanket removal of all trade barriers in the interest of establishing a free market as the arbiter of national production and international trade decisions. Even the advocates of strategic trade policy such as Paul Krugman (1987, 1986, 1979) adhere to the principle of comparative advantage. They argue that large trading countries are sometimes able to obtain additional national benefits from international markets through strategic governmental policies such as reducing import prices (by increasing import quotas) or increasing export prices (by limiting the volume of exports). In strategic trade theory, the purpose of the EEP is to attack the EC's protectionist policy of subsidizing exports. The objective is to eliminate the distortions of free trade and thus allow the principle of comparative advantage to work (private communication from Ivan Roberts, Australian Bureau of Agricultural and Resource Economics, October 19, 1990).

This is precisely the logic that liberal economists have used in support of the EEP. They argue that it is a short-term policy designed to force the European Community to negotiate the elimination of farm export subsidies that distort free trade in agriculture—hence the description of the EEP as a bargaining lever in the Uruguay round of GATT. U.S. policy makers have even offered to discontinue the EEP if the community agrees to phase out its farm export subsidies. The stated objective is free trade in agriculture; beneficiaries would be the United States and other major nonsubsidizing agricultural exporters such as Argentina, Australia, and Canada. There would be losers, however. Many small-scale grain growers in Europe, for example, would be unable to compete and would be forced off their farms, with adverse electoral implications for European governments.

Mercantilist Trade Policy

The term mercantilism tends to invite ridicule and derision from contemporary liberal economists, who associate it with protectionism and relegate it to the history of European trading states during the seventeenth and eighteenth centuries (Viner, 1969:66–67). There is no corpus of academic thought which elaborates a mercantilist theory of trade. All the same, this is not to say that governments do not practice mercantilist policies or

[17]

that such policies lack coherence or purpose. In fact certain mercantilist principles of international trade have traditionally guided government policy makers. According to Edmund Dell (1987:169), an ex-secretary of state for trade in the British government, there are two such principles: that national economic security is a primary goal of nation-states and that it is the responsibility of the state to guarantee economic security.

Dell (1987:ix,3) argues that despite the unwillingness of economists to acknowledge the overriding importance of national economic security as a policy objective, this principle has guided governments for over two hundred years. Mercantilism has prevailed over liberal economic thought in trade negotiations and in determining governmental support for national firms engaged in trade competition. Dell (1984:195) points out that governments plan and organize their economies to guarantee national security. They protect basic industries such as steel, energy, and agriculture; stockpile strategic materials; and subsidize industries—all toward this end.

Mercantilism assumes a Hobbesian state of nature in which conflict and uncertainty characterize international economic relations. No government, therefore, can afford to rely on such an artifact as an automatic, self-regulating mechanism (an invisible hand) or on systemic equilibrium to guarantee its national economic security. Even the founder of classical liberal economic thought, Adam Smith, allowed for national security considerations in economic policy making, as when he supported the seventeenth-century Navigation Acts of Parliament, which required the carriage of British cargo on British ships despite the fact that it involved significantly higher costs. Because failure to support the country's shipping would strengthen the naval power of Britain's chief rival—Holland—Smith recognized the need to trade "opulence for power" in economic policy. He also gave agriculture a special place in the English economy, arguing that the "yeomanry of England" should be "rendered as secure, as independent, and as respectable as law can make them" (Smith, 1947:372).

The classical mercantilist doctrine stressed the importance of a country's trade balance, or current account. It was through achieving a surplus in the current account of its balance of payments that a country accumulated its stock in money. Building a large surplus of gold and silver and, later, the pound sterling and the U.S. dollar demonstrated a country's wealth and political independence.

Modern mercantilists are prepared to accept that states do benefit from open trading in an expanding world economy. They insist, however, that there are circumstances in which trade is a zero-sum game. Nevertheless, contemporary mercantilists do not insist on government restrictions on imports. They are even prepared to accept that there are circumstances in which a trade deficit can be justified as a cost of economic security and welfare. Large and continuing trade deficits are not, however, likely to be acceptable to governments with weak economies whose economic and political autonomy is threatened by their dependence on larger and more powerful states.

Two outstanding examples of states pursuing mercantilist trade policies are Japan and Germany. Their economies are among those that have experienced the strongest growth since World War II, and both countries have stressed the importance of maintaining a positive balance on current account. Japan has been most successful with its mercantilist trade strategy (Rosecrance, 1985; Yoon, 1987). Michael Borrus and his colleagues (1986:91–113) describe how the Japanese government created a competitive advantage for its semiconductor industry by radically and permanently transforming patterns of world trade for the benefit of Japanese national welfare. Moreover, the Japanese government executed this strategy without triggering trade retaliation from the United States, which it effectively shut out of Japanese domestic markets.

The mercantilist position expects conflicts of interest among nations over trade. Mercantilists assume that it is the duty of governments, particularly democratic ones, to protect important domestic economic and political groups; hence free trade can never be the sole consideration in forming trade policy. Dell (1987:184) points out that the benefits of free trade are widely dispersed, whereas its costs are concentrated in certain industries and regions. Each government is thus obliged to formulate trade policy with a view toward protecting certain industries in depressed or economically stagnant areas, especially during conditions of high unemployment and economic stagnation. It must then negotiate to reconcile the resulting trade policy with the policies of other nations. Thus, from the mercantilist standpoint, considerations of national welfare necessarily come into play in all trade negotiations.

As there is no international organization capable of guaranteeing a nation's economic security, governments must retain the capability for protective action. In trade policy, governments must rely on negotiations to advance national interests, and they must possess sufficient power and independence of action to negotiate effectively. Reciprocity, not free trade, is therefore at the heart of the international trading order. Gerard and Victoria Curzon (1976:156–63) explain that it has been so ever since 1947, at least partly because the U.S. Congress has insisted on it.

Dell (1986:128) defines reciprocity as "an exchange of concessions to mutual and equal advantage." From this definition follows the right to withdraw from trade agreements that prove disadvantageous. Reciprocity thus conflicts by definition with the concept of comparative advantage, with its stress on multilateral free trade unfettered by state restrictions and safeguards. Economic statecraft involves restricting trade for the common good—to promote employment, consumer and environmental protection, or national welfare and security.

Paradoxically, although reciprocity is by definition a denial of free trade, it is also the only politically feasible way to move toward freer trade. The reason for this is that the United States, as the largest trading state, will only engage in trade negotiations on that basis. To negotiate with the United States on trade issues, other states must be able to put up obstacles to trade to use as bargaining levers to extract trade concessions from the United States. Reciprocity enables the United States and other countries to bargain for trade concessions while protecting themselves from the dangers that could arise from too rapid a movement toward freer trade.

In both the Reciprocal Trade Agreements Act of 1934 and

the Bretton Woods Agreement at the end of World War II, the United States subscribed to the notion that international commercial treaties should include most-favored-nation (MFN) clauses. This meant that all U.S. tariff cuts were to be reciprocated by trading partners. The GATT itself is predicated, at least in part, on the principle of reciprocity, not free trade. Largely shaped by the United States, it insists on equal trading rights and obligations for all signatories. The principle of reciprocity is contained in Article XXVIII, paragraph 2(a): "the binding against increase of low duties or of duty-free treatment shall, in principle, be recognized as a concession equivalent in value to the reduction of high duties" (General Agreement on Tariffs and Trade, 1969:49).

During the 1950s and 1960s, the United States deviated from the principle of reciprocity in order to contain Soviet and Chinese expansion in Western Europe and Asia. It tolerated the adoption of Article XXIV in the GATT, which allowed the formation of customs unions and free trade areas, despite the conflict with the most-favored-nation principle. This accommodation gave legal recognition to the formation of the European Community in the context of GATT. Once the U.S. security objective of rebuilding the economies of its Western European allies and Japan had been achieved, however, the traditional American policy of trade reciprocity was restored. Jagdish Bhagwati and Douglas Irwin (1987:123) explain this development as an instance of "diminished giant" syndrome and an overvalued dollar combining with the historical appeal of mercantilism. By its second term, the Reagan administration was openly promoting reciprocity, arguing for fair trade, and demanding equal access to foreign markets. This eventually led Congress to demand "full reciprocity," meaning equality of access to individual sectors of foreign economies as well as the elimination of U.S. trade deficits with major trading partners.

William Cline (1982) argues that U.S. trade reciprocity has taken a new, more "aggressive" form, which he illustrates with a quotation from Senator Robert Dole: "Reciprocity should be assessed not by what agreements promise but by actual results—by changes in the balance of trade and investment between ourselves and our major economic partners" (*New York Times*, January 22, 1982). What sets this version of trade reciprocity apart is what is termed *aggressive retaliation*: the threatened withdrawal of trade concessions from trading partners thought to be prospering at the expense of the United States. Cline (1982:28) considers aggressive retaliation a "high risk strategy" because the withdrawal of trade concessions can have unforeseen consequences. It might achieve its objective but it could provoke a trade war.

Judith Goldstein and Stephen Krasner (1984) argue for the strategy of trade retaliation as the only way the United States can counteract unfair practices. They recommend an American "tit-for-tat" strategy against countries that violate GATT rules. Although Goldstein and Krasner are mistaken in asserting that "trade distorting" practices of other states did not threaten the United States until the 1960s and that American interests necessarily coincide with a liberal trading order, there is substance to their argument that such a retaliatory strategy could be successful. The United States' enormous resources make it particularly able to fight a retaliatory trade battle. As Dell (1986:135) points out, the United States may even believe that in such a trade battle it cannot lose.

Such a strategy has its dangers, however. A tit-for-tat strategy tends to assume a two-country model that ignores the difficulty of identifying the first "tat" and the likelihood that other countries would also be hurt by the "tit" and themselves retaliate. Furthermore, many countries would not necessarily agree with the U.S. interpretation of GATT rules, believing it to be self-serving. Trade warfare, which could threaten the world trading order, is a real possibility.

Mercantilist Objectives in U.S. Farm Trade Policy

In the mercantilist approach to trade, increasing export market share is a perfectly legitimate, indeed important, national objective. The Export Enhancement Program is designed to restore America's share in world grain markets by subsidizing the export sales of U.S. grain. G. E. Schuh (1984) as well as Schuh and Cleveland (1986) argue that subsidizing grain exports can improve American industrial and agricultural competitiveness and the allocation of national resources because food is a "wage good." In other words, low food prices translate into higher real incomes for American workers, which in turn make it possible to keep wages relatively low, improving the international competitiveness of both manufactured and farm products.

The Export Enhancement Program also yields what is called a "second-best" gain. Many secondary industries such as textiles, automobiles, and steel have to be highly protected if they are to compete with imports. From the standpoint of the competitiveness of the whole economy, the "first-best" strategy would be to reduce government support for these industries, but this choice is not feasible for reasons of employment, regional growth, and politics. The second-best strategy is to subsidize export industries (including grains) to partially compensate for the costs of protecting secondary industries. That federal farm outlays are only 1 percent of the total budget—while agricultural production, food, and fiber contribute between 16 and 17 percent to the country's gross national product and are the country's single largest merchandise foreign exchange earner—readily demonstrates the value of this second-best good.

Subsidized exports of EC grain to international markets have forced the United States to retaliate to maintain its traditional markets for American producers. The highly regulated EC system of export subsidies automatically increases the payments to grain producers and exporters when they are faced with low prices offered by competing trade rivals such as the United States. It takes into account the U.S.-EC exchange rates, the export subsidies of trading rivals, changes in the weather, world production, and world prices. Because this EC export policy largely insulates European producers and exporters from the adverse effects of fluctuations in the U.S. dollar exchange rate, the U.S. farm loan rate, and levels of U.S. and world grain production, changes in U.S. domestic farm budgetary or monetary policy cannot in themselves enable the United States to recapture and retain markets. Only an offensive weapon like the EEP seems likely to defeat the EC's offensive.

Yet critics of the EEP argue that the U.S. objective of increasing market shares, as opposed to merely disposing of accumulated grain stocks to restore balance in world grain markets, will have adverse consequences for all grain-exporting countries. The large U.S. and EC export subsidies have depressed world grain prices. Because grain producers in most exporting countries now depend on some form of governmental support to sustain the profitability of their production, U.S. and EC export subsidies have forced other governments to increase support for their producers, inevitably increasing political tensions as well. The minister of state for the Canadian Wheat Board, for example, justified a large subsidy payment under the Canadian Western Grains Stabilization Act of 1987 by the necessity of maintaining Canada's own grain market share in the face of the U.S.-EC subsidy war.

The fear that the U.S.-EC subsidy war could lead to a spiraling general trade war lacks foundation. It is based on historical parallels with events leading to the Great Depression of the 1930s. In fact most liberal political economists avoid serious discussion of market-sharing objectives by projecting a gloomy future from that past. They regard the alternative to an international consensus achieved through GATT as protectionism, which, unchecked, could lead to pernicious national trade policies, the collapse of the world trading system, and world depression.

Susan Strange (1985) has attacked what she regards as the liberal myths that protectionism was responsible for the Depression and that tariff reductions were primarily responsible for postwar growth in the world economy. She speculates that the causation is very likely reversed—that is to say, that prosperity made trade liberalization possible. Strange also challenges the widespread assumption that protectionism threatens peace and world order, noting that there are few examples either of states deliberately engaging in trade wars or competing for the shares of third markets or of major international conflicts attributable to the protectionist policies of rival commercial powers (1985:244–45).

The Export Enhancement Program has not triggered a trade war because, despite the formation of trading blocs, the United

States and the EC are highly interdependent in mutual invest-ments. In industrial products in particular, there are so many American trade partners in Western Europe and vice versa that the two bloc's industrial and service sectors are partially inte-grated (private communication from E.-O. Czempiel, Johann Wolfgang Goethe-Universität, November 13, 1990). An esti-mated 45 percent of American capital currently invested abroad is in equity ownership within Europe (Agnelli, 1989). General Motors and Ford, for example, have long had production facili-ties of their own in Spain, and U.S. aircraft manufacturers like Boeing can sell their products in Europe regardless of tariff barriers, owing to the 1980 GATT Agreement on Trade in Civil Aircraft, negotiated by the United States, EC, Japan, Canada, and several other countries, which dropped all duties on commer-cial aircraft (General Agreement on Tariffs and Trade, 1985). Moreover, the U.S.-EC trading relationship is highly favorable to the Europeans. In 1985, for example, EC countries had a trade surplus with the United States of $23 billion (compared with Japan's of $40 billion), up from a 1980 deficit of $19 billion.

Germany's position in the European Community is ambiva-lent. In 1986 its trade expanded dramatically, giving it a surplus with the United States of $30 billion dollars. Between January and October 1986, Germany replaced the United States as the world's foremost exporter. German exports for that period were valued at $223 billion while U.S. exports were at $213 billion (*German Tribune*, January 25, 1987:6). By 1987, German firms exported to the United States twice as much as they imported (*German Tribune*, January 18, 1987:1). Furthermore, Germany's manufactured exports to the United States had seventy-five times the value of its farm products exported there, making it unlikely that the German government would jeopardize that lucrative trade in manufactured goods over an U.S.-EC agri-cultural trade dispute. Yet the German government is also ex-tremely reluctant to antagonize its European Community part-ners, with whom two-thirds of its entire trade transpires.

Although the EEP is unlikely to provoke a general U.S.-EC trade war, it does have the potential to give the United States political leverage over the European Community. From a mercantilist perspective, the Export Enhancement Program is primarily a political tool designed to exacerbate tensions within the European Community over EC budgetary policies and thereby persuade the Europeans to reduce agricultural surpluses and discontinue efforts to capture and retain traditional U.S. grain markets. Even some critics have acknowledged that the program has a role to play in combating EC grain subsidies and strengthening the U.S. position in trade negotiations. Steven McCoy (1989), president of the North American Export Grain Association, which represents such firms as Cargill, has testified that the "only legitimate future purposes to be served by the EEP program [are] in offsetting the EC subsidies and serving U.S. negotiating purposes in the context of GATT."

Chapter Two

The European Threat to
American Grain Exports

During the latter half of the nineteenth century, the United States became Western Europe's principal overseas food supplier. American farm output soared. Wheat production increased from 236 million bushels in 1870 to 522 million bushels in 1900, while corn production rose from 1,094 million to 2,105 million bushels. The United States was a debtor country and European countries were creditors. Western Europe was undergoing industrialization, and population was outstripping domestic food supply. The United States needed European industrial products and capital investments. Interest payments from European investments in the United States made dollars available in Europe to pay for American food imports. U.S. exports of wheat and wheat flour to Europe increased from $68 million in 1870 to about $200 million in 1898.

American farm production continued to grow, albeit at a slower rate, from 1900 to 1915. Output rose from an index figure of 87.3 in 1900 to 95.4 in 1910 and 107.8 by 1915 (1910–14 = 100; Congressional Quarterly, 1984:104). Prices for U.S. farm products were high, land values were rising, and there was a heavy European demand for food products during and shortly after World War I. This growth trend in U.S. farm output was suddenly halted, however, in 1919. World War I transformed the

United States into a creditor country. To sustain high levels of food exports to Europe, the United States had the choice of making new loans to European countries or importing more goods from Europe. Washington was prepared to do neither. When wartime loans to the Allied powers were discontinued in June 1919, the financing available for American food exports to Europe dried up, precipitating a disastrous farm depression in the United States beginning in 1921.

Despite the New Deal farm policy of the 1930s, the U.S. farm sector did not begin to recover until the outbreak of World War II. John Cathie (1985) attributes the recovery to the war and to the U.S. government's support for the foreign demand for American food supplies. During and shortly after the war, the American lend-lease program and the Marshall Plan provided financing for the export of U.S. food supplies to Europe. During the late 1940s, the U.S. government provided European governments and Japan with grants and loans for reconstruction, and this, in turn, made it possible for them to buy American agricultural commodities. After the Korean War in the 1950s, the world demand for U.S. farm output declined again. Washington responded with a food aid program based on trade concessions. This U.S. stimulation of foreign demand was successful. The U.S. share of the world grain trade increased from 15.5 percent of the total for the period from 1934 to 1938 to 26.5 percent for the period from 1954 to 1956. The European Community (at that time, West Germany, France, Italy, Belgium, Luxembourg, and the Netherlands) was the largest grain-importing bloc in the world. Grain imports exceeded exports by a margin of about 20 million metric tons annually (one metric ton equals 2,240 pounds), a figure estimated to be about one-fifth of the region's total grain consumption and about one-fourth of total world trade in grain.

Table 2.1 breaks down the European Community's cereal imports by source for the 1958–65 period. The EC's cereal imports from nonmember countries increased 65 percent. The United States was the EC's principal grain supplier; the volume of cereals imported from the United States more than doubled, and by 1965 it constituted 52 percent of the EC's total cereal imports. At the same time, U.S. grain exports to the EC were also signifi-

Table 2.1. EC cereal imports by source (in thousand metric tons)

	Total world imports[a]	%	From all non-EC countries	%	From USA	%	From Canada	%	From Argentina	%
1958			10,893	100	3,506	100	1,671	100	2,506	100
1959	57,450	100	12,309	113	4,869	139	1,575	94	2,393	96
1960	60,471	105	12,740	117	4,640	132	1,727	103	3,229	129
1961	69,699	122	14,071	129	6,224	178	2,058	123	2,105	84
1962	75,386	131	17,176	158	7,322	209	1,634	98	3,876	155
1963	79,424	138	15,475	142	7,208	206	1,818	109	2,977	119
1964	87,289	152	14,851	136	7,328	209	1,509	90	3,692	147
1965			17,998	165	9,428	269	1,643	98	4,535	181

Source: Food and Agriculture Organization, *Trade Yearbook*, 1965.
[a] 1959 = 100 percent.

cant in relation to total American farm exports there. In 1962, for example, the United States exported to the EC farm products (including cotton, tobacco, and vegetable oils) valued at $1.2 billion, of which grain constituted $400 million, or 30 percent. The same percentage obtained in 1964.

The principal EC cereal-importing countries during this period were Germany, Italy, and the Netherlands; Table 2.2 shows their cereal imports from within the community and outside. Although their imports from within the European Community increased, all three countries met their cereal requirements primarily by importing from outside the EC. In 1965, for example, 59 percent of Germany's cereal imports came from outside the EC; the corresponding figures for Italy and the Netherlands were 94 and 90 percent respectively. Table 2.3 shows total EC cereal imports for the period. Comparing the data in the two tables confirms that the bulk of EC cereal importing was by Germany, Italy, and the Netherlands. In 1965, for example, these three countries were responsible for 2,591 thousand metric tons of the total cereal imports from within the EC, 82 percent of the total of 3,159 thousand metric tons. These three countries were also responsible for cereal imports from outside the EC of 14,627 thousand metric tons, 81 percent of the total of 17,988 thousand metric tons.

[29]

Table 2.2. Major EC cereal importers (unmilled, excluding rice, in thousand metric tons)

	Year	Total cereals imported	
		Within EC	Outside EC
West Germany	1958	616	4,149
	1961	951	4,352
	1962	798	6,723
	1963	905	3,835
	1964	1,396	4,124
	1965	1,834	4,429
Italy	1958	6	1,241
	1961	699	4,337
	1962	161	3,596
	1963	186	4,707
	1964	436	4,352
	1965	407	6,735
Netherlands	1958	166	2,823
	1961	301	3,151
	1962	120	3,679
	1963	95	4,031
	1964	135	3,519
	1965	350	3,463

Source: Directorate General for Agriculture of the EEC Commission, *Newsletter on the Common Agricultural Policy,* January 1967, 11.

Table 2.3. Total EC cereal imports (unmilled, excluding rice, in thousand metric tons)

Year	Within EC	Outside EC
1958	890	10,893
1961	2,238	14,071
1962	1,281	17,176
1963	1,579	15,475
1964	2,380	14,851
1965	3,159	17,998

Source: Directorate General for Agriculture of the EEC Commission, *Newsletter on the Common Agricultural Policy,* January 1967, 11.

Table 2.4. French and EC cereal exports (unmilled, excluding rice, in thousand metric tons)

	Year	Within EC	Outside EC
France	1958	522	881
	1961	1,757	1,859
	1962	963	1,745
	1963	1,211	3,495
	1964	1,644	4,804
	1965	1,969	4,455
EC	1958	784	1,409
	1961	2,287	2,028
	1962	1,298	2,119
	1963	1,599	4,354
	1964	2,196	5,684
	1965	2,992	5,827

Source: Directorate General for Agriculture of the EEC Commission, *Newsletter on the Common Agricultural Policy,* January 1967, 13.

The Growth of French-U.S. Rivalry

The greatest EC cereal-exporting country by far was France, as Table 2.4 shows. In 1965, France was responsible for about 66 percent of all intracommunity cereal exports and 76 percent of community exports to outside countries. That year, too, France became the community's biggest exporter of farm products, with sales accounting for more than one-third of total exports. Between 1958 and 1965, France increased its cereal exports by about 500 percent. The 6.4 million metric tons it exported in 1965 was almost double its 1961 exports. Intracommunity trade in cereals tripled between 1958 and 1965, reaching almost 3 million metric tons. More than 10 percent of all internal EC trade in farm products that year was in cereals. France supplied nearly 2 million metric tons, or 66 percent, of the community's total trade in cereals.

France's exports outside the community in 1965 accounted for almost 4.5 million metric tons of the community's total of 5.8

Table 2.5. EC cereal export recipients (unmilled, excluding rice, in thousand metric tons)

	1958	1961	1962	1963	1964	1965
United Kingdom	570	490	299	686	803	762
Egypt	354	—	—	—	—	71
Switzerland	72	237	315	551	610	800
Senegal	120	143	134	143	153	143
Mainland China	1	230	486	814	500	12
Poland	1	19	177	670	593	423
Algeria	—	103	106	63	67	231
Austria	9	7	16	37	251	353
Spain	—	62	2	252	721	483
Morocco	—	119	89	27	147	100
Hungary	—	—	51	238	65	92
Denmark	57	173	199	228	475	188
East Germany	—	—	—	—	170	958
Czechoslovakia	1	—	—	25	126	241
Sweden	12	5	40	57	53	29
Iran	—	—	—	1	129	60
Portugal	30	26	—	62	42	106

Source: Directorate General for Agriculture of the EEC Commission, *Newsletter on the Common Agricultural Policy*, January 1967, 12.

million, or about 77 percent. Recipient countries are given in Table 2.5. Cereal exports to non-EC countries increased significantly between 1958 and 1965—from 1,409 thousand metric tons to 5,827 thousand metric tons. Most of this increase occurred after 1961. Wheat exports increased the most, from 664 thousand metric tons to 3,883 thousand metric tons (almost 600 percent). The biggest importer of EC wheat during this period was the United Kingdom, followed by Switzerland and Senegal. The Eastern European countries and China became major customers for surplus EC wheat during this period, and large quantities of wheat also went to North Africa, especially Egypt, Algeria, and Morocco. The principal importers of EC fodder grain (livestock feed) were Switzerland, Spain, Austria, Denmark, and the United Kingdom, in that order.

During the 1970s, a dramatic transformation in EC cereal production was in the making. Whereas in 1968 the EC was a net importer of 15.1 million metric tons of grain, in 1982 it was a net exporter of 12 million metric tons (Australian Bureau of Agri-

Table 2.6. Market share of wheat exports (in percentages)

	1970/ 71	1975/ 76	1980/ 81	1981/ 82	1982/ 83	1983/ 84	1984/ 85	1985/ 86
United States	35.8	43.1	42.5	44.7	37.3	35.4	32.9	26.0
France	5.7	11.9	13.8	12.3	12.2	12.7	16.2	17.7
Canada	21.1	16.6	16.8	17.2	20.0	19.8	16.7	17.5
Australia	16.1	11.8	9.9	10.2	7.6	9.6	13.6	16.6
Argentina	1.8	4.3	4.0	3.3	7.0	8.8	6.9	6.3

Source: Dale E. Hathaway, *Agriculture and the GATT: Rewriting the Rules* (Washington, D.C.: Institute for International Economics, 1987), 46.

Table 2.7. Market share of wheat and coarse grains exports (in percentages)

	1970/ 71	1975/ 76	1980/ 81	1981/ 82	1982/ 83	1983/ 84	1984/ 85	1985/ 86
United States	35.0	50.3	51.8	49.8	46.2	44.4	40.8	32.0
France	8.0	9.5	9.6	9.2	10.2	10.5	12.5	14.0
Canada	14.6	10.7	9.8	12.0	14.0	12.8	9.9	11.8
Australia	10.8	7.7	5.6	6.4	4.4	7.4	9.6	11.0
Argentina	9.1	6.3	8.5	7.0	9.4	9.7	8.1	8.2

Source: Dale E. Hathaway, *Agriculture and the GATT: Rewriting the Rules* (Washington, D.C.: Institute for International Economics, 1987), 48.

cultural and Resource Economics, 1985:174). This transformation means imports were reduced by about 30 million metric tons while exports increased to approximating one-fifth of the community's entire production. France accounted for most of the change.

Tables 2.6 and 2.7 show the sharp increase in French cereal exports. France's share of the world market for wheat increased from 5.7 percent in 1970/71 to 17.7 percent in 1985/86, while the U.S. share of the world wheat market declined from a high of 44.7 percent in 1981/82 to 26 percent in 1985/86. World exports of wheat and coarse grains followed a similar pattern. The American share declined from a peak of 51.8 percent in 1980/81 to 32 percent in 1985/86. In contrast, the French share rose from 8 percent of the total market in 1970/71 to 14 percent in 1985/86.

French grains, especially soft wheat, supplied to both the EC

Figure 2.1. U.S. and EC grain imports and exports (rice excluded). From USDA, *Agricultural Outlook*, July 1985.

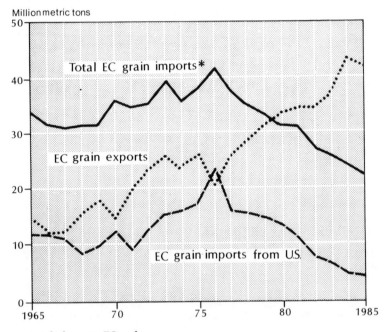

*Includes intra-EC trade.

and outside countries had displaced American exports. Reed Friend (1985), an economist with the U.S. Department of Agriculture (USDA), attributes this shift to both increasing European wheat production (averaging 3.1 percent annually from 1960 to 1985) and the rising value of the U.S. dollar (which has increased the price of American grain). At 4.5 million metric tons, EC grain imports from the United States in 1985/86 were less than one-third of the average during the mid-1970s. Figure 2.1 shows the declining EC grain imports from the United States and other countries and the rising community grain exports for the 1965–85 period, and Figure 2.2 illustrates the reversal in the percentage shares of the world wheat flour market between the

Figure 2.2. U.S. and EC wheat flour exports as shares of world markets. From *Agra Europe*, September 2, 1988, E4.

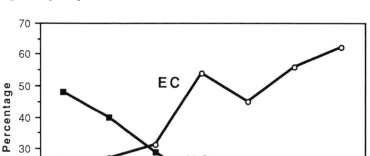

EC and the United States from 1962 to 1986. France of course dominated those EC wheat and wheat flour exports, averaging between 60 and 80 percent of the EC totals.

EC Support for French Exports

This major growth of French cereal exports was supported by the EC's Common Agricultural Policy and the European Agricultural Guidance and Guarantee Fund (EAGGF) was the key to that support. In 1962 the supreme policy-making body of the EC, the Council of Ministers, decided to establish the EAGGF as a means of financing the community's entire common farm policy. The fund provides, among other things, both price supports and export rebates (or refunds) for all common market agricultural products. Under the price support rules, the council annually sets the support prices (the minimum price paid to producers) for products in the community. When the price for farm products in EC national markets falls below the support price levels, the community intervenes by purchasing the products at

[3 5]

the higher support prices. To dispose of surplus agricultural production on world markets, the fund also provides cash rebates (called restitution payments or export refunds) to exporters to make up the difference between high national prices in the European Community and lower world prices.

Community grain prices are primarily designed to guarantee a minimum standard of living for farmers. The EC has aimed its commodity-pricing policy at raising the relatively low living standards in predominantly agricultural regions such as areas of France south of the Loire and west of the Rhone, Corsica, southern Italy, Sardina, and Sicily, characterized by small, undercapitalized farms underequipped with tractors and other modern equipment. Even in the more prosperous farming regions such as areas of Belgium, the Netherlands, and Germany, there is a substantial income disparity between industrial wage earners and most farmers, which the northern EC governments want to reduce.

Sicco Mansholt, Commission of the European Communities vice-president and author of the Mansholt plan, which formed the basis of the community's Common Agricultural Policy, had aired the contradictions inherent in the EC's commodity-pricing policy. Acknowledging that farmers' incomes could be raised by fixing higher prices for commodities, he had warned, however, of the concomitant risks of creating "useless surpluses" of certain commodities and losing millions "down a bottomless pit through relying on price-support and stockpiling" (*European Community*, November 1967:7). In his view, there were only two ways to close the income gap between industrial workers and farmworkers—support commodity prices or restructure farming in the community—and the first entailed excessive waste and cost. Mansholt had argued for the second solution, pointing out that there were too many uneconomic, small-scale farms. To raise farmers' incomes, he thought it necessary to increase the number of medium-sized farms (those between 25 and 125 acres) and, by implication, eliminate the smaller ones.

The European Council of Ministers chose largely to ignore Mansholt's recommendation and to rely on support prices. To guarantee minimum returns to producers, even the numerous

Figure 2.3. The EC system of grain price support. From Australian Bureau of Agricultural and Resource Economics, *Agricultural Policies in the European Community*, Policy Monograph 1 (Canberra: Australian Government Publishing Service, 1985).

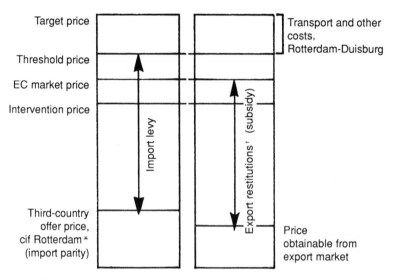

* This price is normally the lowest cif price at which grain can be imported into any EC port, adjusted to a cif Rotterdam basis. Representative world market prices may be somewhat higher than this.

† Restitutions are determined by competitive tender and should reflect the difference between EC market prices obtainable on export markets. After allowing for the costs of freight etc., such export prices may be lower than the third-country offer price.

small-scale, inefficient ones, the council sets commodity prices by geographic region. In each area, grain producers, for example, are assigned specific intervention, target, and threshold prices that provide a floor and a ceiling for both low- and high-cost operations and protect them from competition from outside the EC.

Figure 2.3 illustrates how grain price supports work. At the low end of the scale is the intervention price, which is the price at which the EC must buy grain. It represents the minimum price that producers will receive during any given year, and it is fixed for Ormes, France. Ormes is the largest grain surplus area in the European Community and is theoretically, at least, the lowest-cost producing area. In recent years, however, the EC's intervention procedures have been modified by introducing a buying-in price of 94 percent of the intervention price. The purpose is to equalize the producer price of grain regardless of location within the community. At the high end of the scale is the target price for grain: the maximum price that producers hope to receive. This price is set for Duisburg, Germany, which is deemed to be the community's principal grain deficit area or, theoretically, the highest-cost EC producing area. The target price is the intervention price plus the cost of transport from Ormes to Duisburg plus a market element. The support prices for grain in all other geographic areas of the community are calculated in the same way: intervention price plus the cost of transport from Ormes to the particular area plus a market element. In recent years, however, the EC has instituted a single price for all destinations.

The threshold price is always somewhere between the target price and the intervention price. In effect, it is the equivalent of the target price minus the costs of transport, handling, and other costs for delivery of non-EC grain to community ports. The threshold price is the minimum price at which imported grain may enter the community. The purpose of the threshold price is to ensure that the world price of grain does not undermine the community's market price. When the world price for grain falls below the threshold price, the EC assesses a variable levy equal to the difference between the lowest available import price from outside the EC and the threshold price.

To promote the marketing of surplus EC grain outside the community, restitution payments or export refunds are made in cash to exporters (usually grain companies) to ensure that EC grain is competitive on world markets. Since the community's grain prices are usually well above the world prices, the refunds have grown substantially as exports have increased. According to a recent Organisation for Economic Co-Operation and Development study (1987:165), the estimated price gap between the EC as a whole and world markets is 50 percent or more, although it varies markedly. For example, in 1986 and 1987 the EC's export refunds were very high when world prices were low, but they declined significantly in 1988 when world prices rose, largely because of a North American drought. In 1990 they were high again because world prices returned to low levels.

Export refunds are designed to bridge the gap between the high price that traders often receive on the EC market and the lower price they would ordinarily receive by exporting on the world market. The refunds, and the conditions governing the granting of them, are determined weekly by the EC Cereals Management Committee at its regular Thursday meetings. The committee uses three criteria in setting export refunds: cereal prices in EC export markets, the lowest price offered to importing non-EC countries, and the costs of marketing and transport. More generally, the committee must consider EC and world prices as well as the supply situation to ensure an orderly market for cereals in the community (C.A.P. Monitor, October 1987: 10–19). In other words, the management committee uses the device of export refunds to manage community supply problems by stimulating non-EC demand for the community's agricultural surplus. Export refunds are fixed for any cereal product and can and usually do vary by country of destination.

Differences in the grain support prices within the EC are, however, simply a recognition of the differences in the farm support policies of member states before the European Community was established, when each country set its own prices based on the cost-effectiveness and output of their producers and the political circumstances. In France, the producer's price for wheat for bread per one hundred kilos (220 pounds) was 6.80 units of account (one unit of account = 0.888670 grams of fine gold), whereas the producer's price in Germany was 10.31 units of account. In terms of the arithmetical average of support prices in the EC, the margin of difference was between +20 percent for Germany and −25 percent for France (European Community Information Service, 1959:97–98). Since France was the only producer of surplus grain for export and Germany the principal importer of grains within the EC, it was only natural that these two countries would have considerable weight in determining the community's common grain prices.

In fact, the EC's first common grain price in 1962 rested on a compromise between Germany, with the highest grain support prices, and France, with the lowest. In both countries, national electoral implications were critical (*European Community*, December 1964:3). The German government feared any lowering of the grain price would incense German farmers and provoke electoral opposition. This perception meant that the common prices for grain would have to be higher than the French support prices. Although French farmers and government were happy to have higher prices and increased payments from the European Community to finance the cost of the subsidy, the arrangement nevertheless created difficulties for the government. Higher grain prices tended to stimulate increased production, and the government was already hard pressed to find export outlets for growing grain surpluses.

The French have done well, however. In a confidential document prepared by the Secrétariat general du Comité interministériel pour les questions européennes (SGCI) in 1965, the French government pointed out the advantages of CAP to French farmers and the French economy. The SGCI report argued that the Common Agricultural Policy would have the effect of reducing the competitive capacity of industry in the other member countries, which would be obliged to finance French agricultural surpluses and to give up the advantage of buying on world markets, and it also pointed out that Germany would be contributing $410 million to the EAGGF each year and also paying in about $180 million from levies on agricultural imports into Germany from nonmember countries. Germany would therefore be contributing roughly one-half of the total revenue of the $1.3 billion fund and would only regain a small proportion of that revenue for itself.

The SGCI report estimated that France's net gain from the fund's operation would increase from $65 million for the farming year (July–June) 1964–65 to $122 million for 1967–68 and $164 million for 1969–70. Furthermore, the EC countries would be buying French produce at prices between 30 and 75 percent higher than those obtainable on world markets, which would translate into an advantage worth $47 million in 1964–65 and $79 million in 1969–70. The report concluded that the total

Table 2.8. National contributions and receipts of the
EAGGF guarantee section, 1962–1963

	Contribution (% of total)	Amount received ($ million)	Percentage of total received
France	28.0	24.48	85.20
West Germany	28.0	1.79	6.23
Italy	28.0	1.28	4.46
Netherlands	7.9	0.86	3.01
Belgium	7.9	0.31	1.06
Luxembourg	0.2	0.003	0.01

Source: *European Community*, February 1966:13.
Note: In 1962–63, only one-sixth of the eligible expenditure on the common farm policy was covered by the fund. The sectors covered were grains, pork, eggs, and poultry.

estimated benefit of CAP would be $243 million by 1970. There would also be gains in foreign exchange earnings representing as much as 40 percent of the increase in French foreign exchange reserves in 1964.

Indeed, immediately after the Council of Ministers had agreed on a common grain price in 1967 (retroactive to 1962) the French became the principal beneficiaries of CAP, as Table 2.8 shows. The data indicate that whereas France contributed 28 percent of the payments to the EAGGF,[1] it received over 85 percent of total allocations during 1962–63. The major portion of the funds allocated ($22.3 million out of $28.8 million) were in the form of refunds for exports to non-EC countries. Most of that amount ($21.5 million) was for the export of grains. The second

[1] The EAGGF, also referred to as the FEOGA (Fonds européen d'orientation et de Garantie Agricole), is the instrument through which the CAP is financed. The EAGGF expenditure during the 1980s constituted about two-thirds of the entire EC budget. The bulk of this expenditure, over 90 percent, is for the guarantee section, which finances price support, both through domestic intervention purchases and export refunds. The balance of EAGGF funds (less than 10 percent) is allocated by the guidance section, which finances structural reforms of the agricultural sector. In 1988, cereals accounted for 20 percent of the total EAGGF expenditure, with 12 percent of that figure allocated for export refunds (Commission of the European Communities, 1988:T86).

payment from the EAGGF guarantee section, in 1963–64, followed a similar pattern: France contributed just over 25 percent of the payments while receiving more than 89 percent of the allocations. Export refunds for cereals constituted 79 percent of the allocations from the guarantee section (just over $40 million out of a total of $51 million) (*European Community*, February 1967:11).

France has continued to be the largest recipient of the EAGGF allocation. In 1973 it received 1,194.6 million European currency units (ECUs) compared with 790.6 million ECUs for Germany and only 155.11 million for the United Kingdom. The allocation increased in 1986 to 5,453.0 million ECUs for France, 4.398.4 million for Germany, and 1,999.9 million for the United Kingdom, which amounts to about 25 percent of the total EAGGF allocation for France but only 20 percent for Germany and 9 percent for the United Kingdom (Commission of the European Communities, 1988:T85). The EC Commission released budget figures for net contributions and net receipts for member countries for three years (Table 2.9). Germany and the United Kingdom were major net contributors. In fact, with the exception of France's small net contribution for 1979, Germany and the United Kingdom were the only net contributors to the EC budget.

Although there has been a relative decline in France's net receipts from the community budget since 1981, this has not reduced the political tension in the community over contributions to the EC budget. To the contrary, it has made France less willing to accept Britain's demands for budgetary relief. Any reduction in the United Kingdom's net contribution would cause other countries, including France, to pay more or receive less (Yao-Su Hu, 1979:461).

In addition, France (along with Denmark, Ireland, and the Netherlands) enjoys large trading gains from exporting grain to protected EC markets. These trading gains can be measured by multiplying the amount of wheat by the market prices for wheat in each of the importing EC countries minus a deduction for the differences in monetary exchange rates (monetary compensa-

Table 2.9. Estimated net contributions (−) and receipts (+) from the EC budget (in millions of ECUs)

	1979[a]	1980[b]	1981[c]
West Germany	−1,430	−1,526	−1,750
United Kingdom	−849	−1,512	−1,422
France	−78	+431	+597

Source: H.M. Treasury, "The European Community Budget: Net Contributions and Receipts," *Economic Progress Report*, suppl., October 1982:3.
[a]1 ECU averaged 2.511 deutsche marks, 0.646 pounds, and 5.829 francs.
[b]1 ECU averaged 2.524 deutsche marks, 0.598 pounds, and 5.869 francs.
[c]1 ECU averaged 2.514 deutsche marks, 0.553 pounds, and 6.040 francs.

tory amounts, or MCAs) and a deduction for the cost of transporting grain from the United States to an EC port.[2]

Finally, the French receive a substantial subsidy from the EC, in the form of payments from the EAGGF guarantee section, for the storage of surplus grain. In 1988 the total expenditure for the storage of cereals in the EAGGF budget was 2,007 million ECUs, which was 6.9 percent of the total guarantee expenditure (Commission of the European Communities, 1988:T86). France alone received 50 percent or more of this payment.

British Opposition to the CAP Financial Burden

The principal source of political tension between Britain and the rest of the European Community has been the CAP budget. Christopher Huhne (1985:22) points out that disagreements over Britain's contribution have "overwhelmed and distorted

[2]MCAs are border taxes and subsidies designed to equalize agricultural support prices between EC countries to facilitate free and undistorted movement of farm products.

British concerns and soured official relationships at almost every level from the Prime Minister downwards." Paul Taylor (1982) blames this tension on a lack of British commitment to the European Community beyond short-term economic benefits and on the relative decline of the British economy, for which the EC has become a scapegoat.

The French have always had a strong commitment to the CAP; in fact this commitment formed the basis of the political understanding with Germany that underpinned the 1958 Treaty of Rome, which established the European Community. France took the risk of opening its domestic market to German competition in manufactured goods and was rewarded with a protected common market for its agricultural exports and subsidies for its farmers through the mechanism of the CAP budget. To protect this agreement, France insisted, in the EC negotiations in the 1960s and 1970s, on the completion of the CAP before agreeing to tariff cuts for manufactured goods.

When Britain acceded to the Treaty of Rome in 1973, it was deemed to have agreed to this political understanding between France and Germany. Not only was the cost of the CAP to Britain negligible at the time (because of unusually high world prices for agricultural products), but like Germany, the United Kingdom expected its manufacturing industry to enjoy benefits from access to the common market more than sufficient to offset CAP costs (A. Morgan, 1980:58). But these expected economic benefits did not materialize. On the contrary, British trade in manufactured goods with EC countries has resulted in substantial deficits. In 1978, for example, Britain had a trade deficit with these countries of £2,000 million.

British grievances over the CAP budget stem largely from the failure of its manufacturing industry to benefit substantially from access to the common market. Indeed, Britain's industrial sector has declined relative to other community members since Britain joined the EC. According to Taylor (1982), this disappointment has created a negative attitude toward the European Community in official circles and focused official attention on the short-term budgetary impact of membership. Because the United Kingdom's large net contribution to the CAP budget has been the most tangible symbol of Britain's disappointment, it has become the pivotal issue in British-EC relations.

Britain's relative economic decline since joining the EC only reinforces its disappointment with the economic benefits of membership. For example, from 1962 to 1976, the United Kingdom's per capita gross domestic product (at current prices and exchange rates) declined from second highest to seventh among the nine EC members; between 1962 and 1978, Britain registered the lowest annual rate of growth in the community. Daniel Jones (1980:117) notes, however, that Britain's relative economic decline has been in progress since 1870 and is therefore independent of EC membership. Nevertheless, British perceptions have encouraged governments, both Labour and Conservative, to adopt negative or skeptical attitudes toward the supposed advantages of Britain's involvement in the community.

As early as 1966, the British prime minister, Harold Wilson, spelled out his government's opposition to CAP (*European Community*, May 1966:16): The principal difficulty standing in the way of the United Kingdom's joining the EC was the community's system of agricultural levies (a tax charged on imported foodstuffs to raise their price to the community level). In addition to increasing the cost of living to wage earners by between 2.5 and 3.5 percent per annum, the burden of financing the community would outweigh the benefits to Britain. Perhaps 90 percent of the levies Britain collected would, under the rules of the CAP, be turned over to a central fund administered by the EC Commission. For 1966, for example, the levies would be about 200 million pounds, an amount twice as high as the next highest levy, paid by Germany.

Although CAP financing has changed (from a value-added tax to a percentage of member countries' gross domestic product), successive British governments have continued to voice objections to the budget. Thatcher's Conservative government (1979–91) continued the Labour government's policy of seeking to redress the British grievances. Since 1980, the United Kingdom has received a rebate to reduce its net contribution; for example, Britain's 1985 net budgetary position declined from a minus 3 billion ECUs to a minus 1 billion (*Economist*, 303 [1987]: 23).

[45]

But even after the rebate, the United Kingdom continues to be a substantial contributor.

The French government has consistently opposed any financial reductions in the British contribution to the CAP because it views the CAP as one of its major foreign policy accomplishments. Any reduction in British support for CAP would be a threat to the economic benefits France fought hard to secure from the European Community. Despite those who argue that the United Kingdom has been largely bought off by the rebates it receives, political tensions between the British and the French over CAP contributions do remain, providing the wedge for the American assault on the EC's agricultural export subsidy program.

Chapter Three

The American Response

The contemporary agricultural export subsidy war between the United States and the European Community was an
almost inevitable outcome of the policies adopted by the United
States and the European Community after World War II. The
farm support policies on both sides have produced the same
results: overproduction, stockpiling, and dumping products on
world markets through food aid and concessional sales. Any
difference in policies has been largely one of timing. U.S. farm
policies were largely formulated during the Great Depression; by
the 1940s, they were already stimulating production in excess of
demand. The EC's Common Agricultural Policy did not go into
effect until the early 1960s, and by the late 1970s, production
was in surplus. The EC's export promotion policy roughly paral-
leled that of the United States except that it was adopted during
the 1970s instead of the 1940s. Since both trading blocs had
achieved substantial agricultural surpluses by the 1970s, conflict over shares of world agricultural markets was predictable.

Farm income in the United States between 1860 and 1940 did
depend on foreign markets, but never for more than 20 percent
of the total. After 1940, foreign sales began to climb above 20
percent of gross farm income (Cathie, 1985:17), so that in 1981,
for example, 30 percent of American farm income came from

sales abroad. Whereas before 1940, American farm policy was largely determined by domestic conditions, foreign markets began to drive domestic farm policy after 1940, as the United States emphasized market expansion overseas.

Subsidized sales began to account for a significant share of agricultural trade as the government disposed of large stocks of surplus agricultural products. U.S. support for export sales also stimulated the rise of agribusiness. Cathie (1985:17) estimates that by 1982, the 1 percent of farms with incomes over half a million dollars received two-thirds of total farm income. Fewer companies have come to control increasingly larger shares of the agribusiness market, which now includes retailing and food manufacturing. As a result, manufacturers and suppliers are now influencing farm policy, and the government, in formulating that policy, is expected to protect such potentially conflicting interests as those of farm producer associations, large and small; large international food producing and processing corporations; farm cooperative organizations; and consumer and environmental groups. The government is pressed to pursue multiple, sometimes contradictory policy objectives such as finding outlets for surplus production, increasing production and export earnings, reducing acreage under cultivation, and maintaining levels of employment.

After World War II, the future members of the European Community set about achieving food self-sufficiency and a guaranteed minimum income for farmers. The Common Agricultural Policy was only fully implemented during the mid-1960s. High agricultural support prices set in response to pressure from European farming interests began to stimulate production, the CAP created surpluses of milk, butter, skimmed milk powder, wheat, barley, wine, beef, sugar, and fresh fruit and vegetables. Between 1973 and 1982, EC agricultural production tripled. While food production was increasing by 24 percent, food consumption was only increasing by 8 percent (Engles et al., 1985:i). The value of EC agricultural production jumped from 281 million ECUs in 1973 to 347 million ECUs in 1982, while the value of agricultural products consumed increased only from 298 million to 323 million ECUs. Grain harvests con-

tinually broke production records as the use of chemical fertil-
izers and modern agricultural technology became widespread.
Whereas the community was only 91 percent self-sufficient in
wheat and barley production during the 1972–73 season, it had
achieved 114 percent self-sufficiency in 1984 (Engles et al.,
1985:ii).

Although the United States saw itself being displaced from
its traditional agricultural markets as early as the 1960s, it re-
frained, with one exception, from retaliating against the European Community for what were largely national security reasons. A strong, unified Western alliance to contain the threat of
Soviet expansionism seemed more important than the loss of
agricultural markets. The one exception was the famous "chick-
en war" of the 1960s, which did threaten all trade between the
blocs—and the political unity of NATO as well.

Only in the 1980s did the United States begin to react openly
to the loss of markets. When the EC restricted the imports of
soya (concentrated feeds) and cereal substitutes, which the
United States supplied, the United States responded in 1982 by
trying to break into a traditional European market—Egypt—by
offering a cut-rate price for flour. When the European Community sold butter in traditional U.S. markets at below commercial
prices, the United States retaliated by withdrawing from the
International Dairy Agreement (which sets minimum world
prices for dairy products) so it could sell its dairy surpluses on
world markets at low prices. Since the mid-1980s, the United
States and the European Community have been involved in
what Dale Hathaway (1987:4) describes as "guerrilla trade warfare" in international grain markets, a conflict with the potential
to threaten both political and economic cooperation in the At-
lantic alliance.

The Export Enhancement Program

It was under the Reagan administration that the policy toward
retaliation changed, in response to an alarming decline in U.S.
agricultural exports. From 1979 to 1981, farm exports, a vital

Table 3.1. U.S. agricultural trade balances (in billion dollars)

	1950	1960	1970	1975	1980	1981	1982	1983	1984	1985	1986
Agricultural											
Exports	2.9	4.8	7.3	21.9	41.2	43.3	36.6	36.1	37.8	29.0	26.2
Imports	4.0	3.8	5.8	9.3	17.4	16.8	15.2	16.5	19.3	20.0	21.5
Balance	−1.1	1.0	1.5	12.6	23.9	26.6	21.2	19.6	18.5	9.1	4.8
Nonagricultural											
Balance	2.5	4.4	1.3	−2.9	−51.3	−56.6	−56.4	−80.3	−129.4	−133.8	−167.1
Total											
Balance	1.4	5.4	2.8	9.7	−27.4	−30.0	−35.2	−60.7	−110.9	−124.7	−162.3

Source: "The 1986 Agricultural Outlook," appendix to a statement by Robert L. Thompson, assistant secretary of agriculture for economics, before the House Appropriations Committee's Subcommittee on Agriculture, Rural Development, and Related Agencies, March 12, 1986: 25; and USDA, Economic Research Service, Foreign Agricultural Trade of the United States calendar year 1985 (supplement), July 1986: 1.

component of the overall U.S. trade balance, averaged about 19 percent of total U.S. exports. The net U.S. agricultural trade balance averaged about $17 billion over those same years. The value of U.S. farm exports had increased by 600 percent, from $7.3 billion in 1970 to $43.3 billion in 1981 (Table 3.1). This gain constituted 18.9 percent of all U.S. exports that year. The dramatic increase was largely attributable to two fortuitous circumstances: the fall in the value of the U.S. dollar, which made American farm products more competitive in world markets, and the emergence of the Soviet Union as a major buyer of U.S. grain.

Then, in 1982, a worldwide recession reversed this upward trend (Figure 3.1). Agricultural exports that year dropped to $36.6 billion, or 17.7 percent of total U.S. exports. Net agricultural exports continued to decline during 1983 and 1984 and reached a low of $9.1 billion, or 17.2 percent of total U.S. exports, in 1985. Farm exports in 1985 contributed less than 14 percent of the total value of all U.S. exports, the lowest percentage since 1940. The decline in the agricultural trade balance coincided with the country's worsening overall merchandise trade deficit, which reached a record $162.3 billion in 1986; a large positive agricultural trade balance could no longer be counted on to offset the nonagricultural deficit.

The U.S. share of grain export markets in particular fell dramatically, from 52 percent of the world market in 1981 to 32 percent in 1986. In 1981, the United States sold 48.2 million metric tons of wheat overseas compared with one-half that amount, or 24.5 million metric tons, in 1985. The lower overseas sales also produced a huge grain surplus at home. The silos were filling, and there was concern that there would be insufficient space to store the 1986 surplus grain harvest. The USDA estimated that the cost to the government of buying and storing agricultural surplus products in 1986 would exceed twenty billion dollars, an unprecedented sum. Both government and farmers had a powerful incentive to increase export sales of farm products.

Roberts (Australian Bureau of Agricultural and Resource Economics, private communication, October 19, 1990) suggests that the U.S. grain surplus was as much a result of the rising value of

Figure 3.1. U.S. agricultural trade balance (in billions). From Reed E. Friend, "Agricultural Outlook" (Washington, D.C.: USDA, 1985).

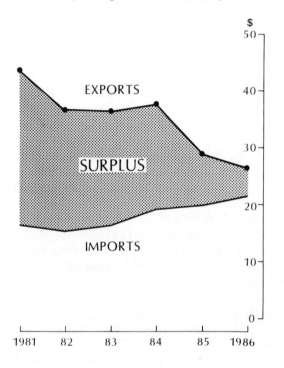

the U.S. dollar, high and inflexible loan rates, and the failure to cut production through area reduction programs as it was a consequence of shrinking foreign markets. Yet however one weighs the causes, the fact remains that the European Community was poised to capture U.S. markets and wage a subsidy war regardless of U.S. monetary and farm policies. The United States responded with the Export Enhancement Program, announced by the USDA in May 1985. Its stated purpose was to enable U.S. exporters to meet prevailing world prices for certain commodities in particular countries. To accomplish this purpose, the program would have to achieve two objectives: expand American farm exports and persuade countries engaged in unfair trading practices to negotiate on agricultural trade problems.

[52]

The Food Security Act of 1985, which was signed into law in December, made the Export Enhancement Program mandatory through fiscal year 1988 and authorized program spending of $2 billion. Continued funding after the initial three years was allocated under the provisions of the Commodity Credit Corporation Charter Act, with expenditures capped at $700 million in fiscal year 1989 and $500 million in fiscal year 1990.

From the EEP's inception until October 1991, 119 export initiatives were approved by the USDA involving 80 countries and twelve commodities (Table 3.2). Total bonuses of the authorized EEP exports were $3,770.9 million, with a gulf or market price of $2,517.1 million. During fiscal 1987, exports under the program constituted 7 percent of the total value of U.S. agricultural exports (up from 3 percent in 1986). Although the program as originally written encouraged the secretary of agriculture to expend at least 15 percent of the funds for export sales of meat and poultry products, wheat exports dominated. In 1988, about 50 percent of all U.S. wheat and flour exports were marketed under the EEP.

In administering the EEP the USDA targets markets supplied by the firms of heavily subsidizing countries—primarily the European Community. Because the preponderance of commodities marketed under the EEP are wheat, flour, and barley and because France is the principal EC grain-exporting country, the EEP's target markets are primarily those supplied by France. Table 3.3 presents data on the main countries targeted for wheat through the end of December 1988. Approximately 62.3 million metric tons of wheat were authorized under the program during this period, and about 51 million tons were sold, accounting for 46 percent of total U.S. wheat exports. The principal areas targeted by the EEP were North Africa, with authorized sales of 17.98 million metric tons; the USSR, with 14.8 million metric tons; and China, with 10.2 million metric tons. In the case of Algeria, for example, the U.S. share of its grain market had fallen from 41 percent in 1979–80 to 16 percent in 1984–85, while the EC had succeeded in increasing its market share from 29 to 59 percent.

The USSR and China were excluded from the program during

Table 3.2. Commodities sold under the EEP as of October 1991

Commodities	Quantity
	Metric tons
Wheat	96,386,441
Barley	10,003,582
Flour[a]	3,091,400
Semolina[a]	53,000
Barley malt[a]	253,339
Sorghum	319,000
Rice	270,610
Feed grains	10,286,482
Poultry feed	188,968
Vegetable oil	713,500
Frozen poultry	204,826
	Head
Dairy cattle	69,773
	Dozens
Table eggs	64,803,844

Source: USDA, Foreign Agricultural Service, "Export Enhancement Initiatives," announcement, April 28, 1989; and communication from James Warden, Branch Chief, Rules, Regulations, and Reports Branch, Commodity Credit Corporation, October 11, 1991.

Note: Sales of wheat, wheat flour, barley, barley malt, and semolina are assigned a specific quantity of bonus certificates, whereas sales of poultry feed, vegetable oil, frozen poultry, dairy cattle, and table eggs are assigned a specific value of certificates instead of a specific quantity.

[a]Grain equivalent.

its first two years of operation, and wheat sales to them suffered as a result. EEP wheat exports to the USSR totaled only 150,000 metric tons, less than 1 percent of the Soviet Union's total wheat imports and a marked drop from the roughly 22 percent the United States had supplied before the EEP (averaging 9 million

Table 3.3. EEP wheat initiatives to major destinations

Recipient bonus country	Period of announcements	Quantity (000 MT)	Sales (000 MT)	Average ($/MT)
Algeria	Jun. 85–Aug. 88	5,200	4,600	35.12
China	Jan. 87–Dec. 88	10,200	10,190	28.77
Egypt	Jul. 85–Dec. 88	5,665	5,136	25.53
India	Apr. 88–Oct. 88	3,000	2,000	21.28
Iraq	Jan. 87–Oct. 87	1,800	1,772	23.13
Jordan	Mar. 86–Mar. 88	1,450	415	32.15
Mexico	Dec. 87–Oct. 88	1,400	1,131	32.14
Morocco	Sep. 85–Dec. 88	5,290	4,170	33.43
Philippines	Jan. 86–Feb. 88	1,850	1,482	21.59
Poland	Jan. 87–Mar. 88	2,500	1,975	40.19
Tunisia	Mar. 86–Feb. 88	1,825	1,075	29.89
Turkey	Oct. 85–May. 86	1,000	755	30.76
USSR	Apr. 87–Dec. 88	14,815	12,805	34.98
Yugoslavia	Apr. 86–Oct. 86	1,400	817	30.31
Total	Jun. 85–Dec. 88	62,332	51,067	31.59

Source: Home-Grown Cereals Authority *Weekly Digest*, February 6, 1989.

metric tons annually for 1981–1985). U.S. wheat exports to China in 1985–86 and 1986–87 amounted to less than 0.9 million metric tons, or only 6.5 percent of total Chinese wheat imports, compared with the previous five-year average of 44 percent of its imports supplied by the United States. It was only after the USSR and China were offered wheat on EEP terms that they resumed importing from the United States on a large scale.

Significant sales of barley have also been made under the EEP. In excess of 7.8 million metric tons have been authorized for sale under the program, and 6.5 million metric tons had been sold as of December 1988—4 million to Saudi Arabia, 700,000 each to Poland and Algeria, 600,000 to Israel, and 500,000 to Tunisia. Approximately 2.23 million metric tons of wheat flour have been allocated under the program since 1985, with 1.2 million of that targeted for Egypt.

All EEP sales are carried out by private U.S. companies, primarily large corporations (see Appendix). The operation of the program is illustrated in Figure 3.2. The EEP is supervised by an interagency governmental review system. Proposals origi-

[55]

Figure 3.2. EEP operational details; proposal through announcement. From USDA, *The Export Enhancement Program: Review and Assessment of Program Criteria and Objectives,* report, May 15, 1989.

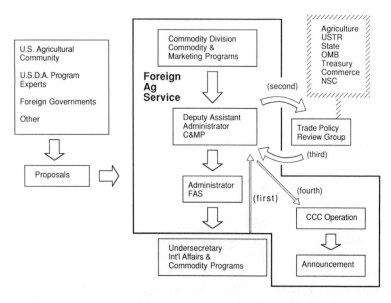

nate from several sources: foreign governments, USDA officials, and the American farming community, which includes grain companies and state grain-marketing boards. Each proposal is forwarded to the USDA's Foreign Agricultural Service (FAS), where it is considered by the appropriate committee; a wheat proposal, for example, would be considered by the Grain and Feed Division. From the FAS, the proposal goes to the undersecretary for international affairs and commodity programs. Once approved by the undersecretary, it goes to the Trade Policy Review Group, which provides input from the departments of State, Commerce, and Treasury; the Office of Management and Budget (OMB); the U.S. trade representative; and the National Security Council. If approved, the USDA announces it. The importers in targeted countries (usually government agencies) may then make a bid to purchase the commodity offered.

After the USDA has announced a bid, U.S. exporting firms

contact prospective foreign buyers and come to a tentative agreement on prices, quantities, and terms of the sale. A prospective U.S. exporting company then submits to the Department of Agriculture a bid for a bonus, or subsidy, to make the sale possible at the price agreed upon with the foreign buyer. The USDA then considers the bid in the light of offers from other U.S. exporters and from competing countries. The competitiveness of the bonus requested for each sale and the sale price are considered in deciding whether to accept the bid. Once the USDA accepts a bid, the sale is completed. After the commodity is delivered to the foreign buyer, the USDA pays the bonus to the U.S. exporter in the form of a commodity from the Commodity Credit Corporation (CCC) stockpile. Exporters receive "generic certificates" of a specified value, with which they or an assignee can claim that amount of any commodity in the CCC inventory.

The largest agribusiness corporations and grain companies are the major recipients of the EEP subsidies. As of late 1991, Cargill, with total bonus value of $689 million, topped the list (see the Appendix); Continental Grain Company was second, with a bonus value of $633 million; Louis Dreyfus Corporation was third, with a bonus value of $504 million. The total number of EEP recipients was 92, with a total bonus value of about $3.8 billion. The program as a whole paid out almost $1.9 billion in export bonuses on $4.4 billion in total sales between May 1985 and mid-1988. This represents average bonuses of about 43 percent of the total value of the EEP exports (U.S. House of Representatives, Committee on Appropriations, 1988:737, 798–99). In 1988, over 60 percent of the value of U.S. wheat and flour exports and about 50 percent of barley exports were supported by the EEP (Crowder, 1989:7).

Conflict over Objectives:
Farm Aid versus Political Tool

The Export Enhancement Program was the product of a compromise agreement between several key farm-state senators—Mark Andrews (R-N.D.), Edward Zorinsky (D-Neb.), and Robert

Dole, the Senate majority leader—and the Reagan administration. The compromise was designed to secure Senate passage of President Reagan's 1985 budget resolution. The senators were displeased with the 1985 farm bill's low price supports. There was a huge inventory of wheat, and they wanted an export subsidy program to control the damage to farmers that they expected the legislation to cause. They knew, for example, that the scheduled drop in price supports for wheat the spring and summer of 1986 would significantly reduce farmers' income. Moreover, even with prices lower, the United States would be competing with EC subsidized exports in world markets.

Senators Andrews and Zorinsky proposed the Export Enhancement Program as a way of disposing of the large wheat inventory by directly combating the EC's export subsidies (Patrick, 1985; private communication from Dan McGuire, ex-director of the Nebraska Wheat Board, January 4, 1991). Senator Andrews argued that export subsidies were more acceptable politically than domestic policy reform as a way of regaining a competitive advantage in world markets. The senators also expected the Export Enhancement Program to raise the price of wheat and thereby improve the image of farmers and strengthen the industry's influence in Congress. A higher price for wheat would, they believed, keep deficiency payments down, lowering the cost of the farm bill and thus neutralizing public opposition to increased farm support payments.

The senators made the EEP the price of their support for the president's 1985 budget package. Senator Dole brokered the deal. He was able to convince the Reagan administration to negotiate because, the Republicans controling the Senate by only a narrow margin, the farm-state senators' support was crucial for passage of the budget. The administration promised the three senators the new two billion dollar program, and in return they cast decisive votes on the president's budget. It passed by one vote (U.S. House of Representatives, Committee on Agriculture, October 10, 1985:161).

The administration may have agreed to establish the program, but it did so without enthusiasm, as was evident soon after the program was announced. The administration took the position that the $2 billion allocated should be spread out over the three years of the program and then successfully sought to reduce the initial authorization to between $1 billion and $1.5 billion. The administration rejected the farmers' across-the-board approach to subsidies and insisted on limiting both the commodities eligible and the markets to be targeted. The criteria were to be established by the cabinet-level Economic Policy Council, made up of representatives from the departments of Agriculture, Commerce, Treasury, Labor, and State and the Council of Economic Advisors plus the U.S. trade representative. The council laid down four limitations: an EEP sale must increase U.S. exports above what they would have been without the program; it must target a specific-country market to challenge competitors who overtly subsidize their exports; it must contribute to the overall economy; and it must not cause budget outlays beyond what would have occurred without the program.

From the beginning, all parties affected by the program strove to modify it or to use it for their own objectives, with conflict an inevitable result. The Reagan administration and the USDA, though saddled with a subsidy program they did not want, moved quickly to use the EEP as a surplus disposal program for wheat. Once the wheat surplus was eliminated in 1987, the administration continued to use the EEP as a trade policy weapon against EC subsidies and as a bargaining chip in the Uruguay round of the GATT talks.

The large agribusiness corporations such as Cargill consistently opposed the program from the beginning. They subscribe to liberal trade doctrine and argue that export subsidies are not an effective policy instrument. From their point of view, there should be a single price for domestic and foreign customers for farm commodities. The EEP, as they see it, only encourages customers to look toward the U.S. government instead of the grain companies (in other words, the market) when considering grain purchases. According to Cargill, this tends to discourage rather than stimulate export sales. The large grain companies rely on the movement of grain from buyer to seller in world markets free of governmental control. Cargill joined various consumer groups—the Consumer Federation of America, the

Consumers Union, and the Community Nutrition Institute—in pressing for an end to U.S. subsidies of overseas grain sales (Anthan, 1988:13).

Farm-state congressmen and senators representing grain producers tend to support the Export Enhancement Program, and some wish to expand it to include all farm commodities. They take the position that the EEP has worked to increase U.S. grain exports, raised wheat prices and thus farmers' income, and lowered farm program costs. They believe anything that keeps the market price firm helps farmers and stimulates export sales. Some producer advocates argue that the EEP should also be used to capture non-EC markets such as those belonging to Canada, Australia, and Argentina. In other words, the program should be used to go after all markets, says Dan McGuire, formerly of the Nebraska Wheat Board (private communication, January 4, 1991).

Producer advocates of the EEP criticize it for being too cumbersome to be truly responsive to sales opportunities. They argue that it is too slow. The interagency authorization process is a classic case of government-induced complexity in conflict with real-world conditions. For example, the OMB is involved in EEP decisions for budgetary reasons, and the State Department and the National Security Council are involved for foreign policy reasons. These and other agencies must all sign off on any export subsidy decision. When Norwegian officials sought approval for an export subsidy sale of U.S. wheat in October 1990, they had to wait for authorization until the end of December despite the fact that Norway was a cash customer in need of prompt clearance. Farm advocates want the cumbersome review process removed.

Congress and the administration clashed over the purpose of the EEP. Farm-state senators and congressmen took the position that the purpose of the program should be to move surplus farm products into world markets as expeditiously as possible. To this end, they believed the entire two billion dollars worth of surplus agricultural commodities owned by the CCC should be made available as a subsidy to U.S. exporters to expand U.S. farm sales during the first year of the three-year program, and that more funding should be then allocated as needed. Further-more, they thought the subsidy should be applied across the board, to all commodities and all countries.

While the farm-producer organizations and their political supporters in Congress favored an export promotion program, they also had misgivings; some even argued that the program jeopardized existing farm exports by alienating traditional U.S. customers who were excluded. Under congressional pressure, the program was modified in 1987 to include all countries with the exception of Japan, the newly industrializing countries of the Pacific basin (where the United States was running large trade deficits), and other competing agricultural exporting coun-tries such as Brazil and Argentina (U.S. House of Representa-tives, 1987). But the program remained a targeted one, and the way it was targeted reveals the administration's underlying ob-jective.

In congressional hearings in late 1985, farm-state representa-tives expressed their dissatisfaction, arguing the EEP would not succeed in winning back lost U.S. markets and could indeed result in the loss of existing ones. They pointed to what they saw as a contradiction in the program: the selective targeting of endangered markets. Daniel Amstutz, the undersecretary of the USDA International Affairs and Commodity Program, acknowl-edged that the EEP targeted European Community markets be-cause the agricultural exports were highly subsidized, giving the example of EC-subsidized French wheat and flour sales. For this reason, the first six EEP initiatives were all directed at French-dominated markets: Algeria, Egypt, Morocco, Yemen, and Turkey.

Congressmen questioned the wisdom of focusing on just those countries, noting that France's most significant penetration of traditional U.S. agricultural markets was not in the Mediterra-nean or in Francophone Africa but in the Soviet Union. Table 3.4 contains data presented at the congressional hearings in support of their contention. These data indicate a significant increase in EC (mostly French) wheat sales to the Soviet Union, from 700,000 metric tons in 1979–80 to 6.1 million metric tons in 1984–85. Even more alarming to the congressmen was the fact

Table 3.4. The EC's wheat market
penetration of the Soviet Union (in
million metric tons)

1984–85	6.1
1983–84	3.6
1982–83	3.4
1981–82	1.7
1980–81	0.9
1979–80	0.7

Source: U.S. House of Representatives, Committee on Agriculture, *Review of the Export Enhancement Program Announced by the U.S. Department of Agriculture,* 99th Cong., 1st sess., serial 9916, 1985:192.

that in 1980–81, at the time of the U.S. grain embargo against the USSR, the Soviet Union had purchased 3 million metric tons of wheat from the United States, whereas they had bought less than 1 million metric tons from the EC. By 1984–85, that 3 : 1 U.S. advantage in market share had evaporated, and the EC and the United States were at parity, each selling 6.1 million metric tons of wheat to the USSR.

Subcommittee Chairman Berkley Bedell questioned Amstutz about the logical consistency of USDA's targeting policy, pointing out that the USSR was the European Community's largest market for wheat, taking approximately 30 percent of the EC's total wheat exports. Whereas, according to 1985 estimates, Algeria would receive 495,000 metric tons of EC wheat; Egypt, 750,000 metric tons; Morocco, 300,000; Yemen, 20,000; and Turkey, 170,000 metric tons the USSR would receive 8 million metric tons of EC wheat. How, Bedell wanted to know, could the USDA refuse to include the USSR as an EEP target when it was the EC's largest single market for subsidized wheat sales and yet include other EC client states receiving a fraction of the EC's sales to the USSR?

Amstutz responded that the Soviet Union was excluded from the Export Enhancement Program because selling subsidized U.S. wheat to the USSR would injure so-called nonsubsidizing wheat exporters such as Argentina, Australia, Canada, and Brazil. The USDA did not want to alienate these countries because the United States needed their support to pressure the EC to discontinue subsidizing agricultural exports. Clearly, the administration's primary objective for the EEP was not to stimulate the expansion of U.S. farm exports but to punish the highly subsidized agricultural exporting countries of the EC by increasing the cost to them of subsidizing exports. What the Reagan administration wanted to achieve was a rule change in the GATT to make it more difficult for all countries to use export subsidies.

Suzanne Early, the assistant U.S. trade representative for agricultural affairs and commodity policy of the Office of the U.S. Trade Representative, supported this interpretation. Testifying before the Congress in 1985, she stated that EC countries will only begin to reassess their agricultural export subsidy policies when the costs of these policies begin to rise (U.S. House of Representatives, Committee on Agriculture, 1985:194–95). Early asserted that if the U.S. dollar were to come down and if the price of U.S. farm products in world markets were to decline, the EC would begin to feel the cost of export subsidies. Figure 3.3 shows the decline in the value of the U.S. dollar from 1985 to 1987 in terms of the value of the EC's international unit of account, the ECU. The administration viewed 1985 as a strategic time to launch the Export Enhancement Program because it was projecting a decline in the value of the U.S. dollar. That year the average value of the ECU relative to the U.S. dollar was 1.32 ECUs. During 1986 and 1987, the value of the U.S. dollar in ECUs did decline by 39 percent, to 0.81 on April 29, 1988.

Richard Fritz, the director of market analysis of U.S. Wheat Associates, also testified that the Export Enhancement Program was designed to end the EC's export subsidization (U.S. House of Representatives, Committee on Agriculture, 1985:62–63). He gave the example of the increased export refunds the EC was forced to make in response to EEP offers to Yemen, Morocco, and Algeria in 1985. To outcompete the United States and to complete its sales of wheat and flour to these countries, the EC was forced to increase its export subsidies substantially. In conjunction with a lower U.S. dollar, an expanded Export Enhance-

[63]

Figure 3.3. Minimum and maximum values of the dollar in terms of the ECU. From Commission of the European Community, *The Agricultural Situation in the Community: 1987 Report* (CEC: Brussels, 1988), 26.

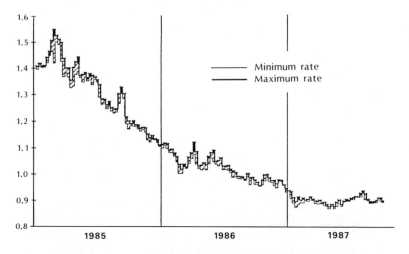

ment Program would lead to large EC export refunds, which in turn would increase the cost of the Common Agricultural Policy to the European Community. Fritz concluded that the extent to which the Europeans were committed to continued heavy subsidization of the CAP would determine when they would come to the bargaining table and negotiate reductions in exports subsidies.

Therefore, the expansion of U.S. exports was only a secondary objective of the EEP. The United States would not have to take back markets lost to France, for example, in order to achieve its principal objective for the Export Enhancement Program; all it needed to do was increase the cost to the European Community of retaining existing markets. A significantly increased level of EC export refunds would add to the already onerous financial burden of European support for the CAP. With political tension within the European Community over the CAP already high, the administration hoped the additional pressure would force the EC to negotiate the elimination of their export subsidies.

Several farm-state congressmen expressed their annoyance at the administration's political objective for the EEP and reaffirmed their position that expanding U.S. sales in world markets and thereby giving hard-pressed farmers some economic relief by raising the prices for their products should be the primary objective. They also declared their skepticism about the usefulness of the EEP as a short-term trade policy tool to win changes in GATT rules and persuade President Mitterrand to negotiate a reduction in French export subsidies (U.S. House of Representatives, Committee on Agriculture, 1985:196).

Nevertheless, the Reagan administration stuck to its strategy. In July 1987, the United States put forward a proposal in the Uruguay round of the GATT talks calling for the complete elimination of all agricultural export subsidies, direct and indirect. The proposal amounted to a fundamental reform of domestic policies that distort trade by excessive support of agriculture. There were three basic components of the proposal. The first was to freeze and then completely phase out over ten years all subsidies affecting agricultural trade. The second was to stop the spread of new market access barriers. The third was to harmonize international food, plant, and animal health regulations to minimize their adverse effects on the flow of trade. The proposal was put before the GATT Agricultural Negotiating Group meeting in Geneva.

President George Bush committed himself to the EEP and to the Reagan administration's long-term international agricultural reform policy. Bush's approval of the subsidized sale of 1.5 million metric tons of wheat to the Soviet Union under the EEP in May 1989 communicated the U.S. determination to keep up the pressure on the EC. Both the secretary of agriculture, Clayton Yeutter, and the U.S. trade representative, Carla Hills, backed continued U.S. efforts to persuade the EC to completely eliminate "trade-distorting" farm subsidies. After the United States failed to reach agreement with the EC countries on agricultural reform at the GATT trade negotiations held in Montreal in December 1988, however, the Bush administration expressed a willingness to consider short-term measures leading to long-term reform. Nevertheless, Hills, like Yeutter when he was her predecessor, underscored the strategic importance of "the credible threat of retaliation" as a trade policy tool for U.S. "market-opening efforts" (quoted in Schaffer, 1989). From the U.S. perspective a settlement of the grains issue was the minimum measure of success in GATT agricultural negotiations. Grains are the key, asserts former under secretary of agriculture Dale Hathaway (1987:21, 27), because the land area devoted to the production of grains (600 million hectares) far exceeds that devoted to any other crop; grain is an essential foodstuff in many countries; the price of grains is critical to the production costs of livestock, dairy, and poultry and therefore in the trade of these commodities; and grain is a vital component in the export earnings of the United States, France, Australia, Canada, and Argentina.

Chapter Four

The Grain Subsidy War

Shortly after the Export Enhancement Program was inaugurated in 1985, the French government produced a confidential internal document on its significance. The report was issued in September 1985 and was entitled "Summary of Grain Exports 1984/1985 and Perspectives for 1985/1986 in the Context of an American Offensive in World Markets." It sought to explain France's exceptional grain exports in 1984–85, and it evaluated the prospects for future French grain exports in the light of the EEP.

Among the favorable factors leading to the expansion of French grain exports, the report singled out the excellent harvest, especially of wheat. The 1984 harvest of 30 million metric tons exceeded the 1983 harvest by 8 million metric tons, and the poor harvest in the Soviet Union enabled France to expand its grain exports. The USSR was forced to import an additional 7 million metric tons of grain, half of which was supplied by France. Other positive factors were the difficulties the United States had in shipping its grain to Morocco and Tunisia and the disruptive credit problems those countries were experiencing. France had no such credit difficulties because of its government's efforts to provide agrifood credit to those countries. France was thus able to renew an agricultural credit agreement with Egypt, conclude a three-year credit agreement with Morocco in May 1985, and propose an extension of its 1984 trade agreement with Tunisia in February 1985.

The report noted that the development of French grain sales was particularly strong in wheat but also in barley. Wheat exports increased by 5 million metric tons, from 14 million metric tons in 1983–84 to 18.7 million in 1984–85, an increase of 35 percent; and the increase occurred in Europe and the Third World. The expansion of sales in Europe was in part due to an increase in the use of wheat as animal feed, made possible by prices low relative to those of other grains. The increase in French exports to world markets was attributed to increased demand as well as to favorable price/quality ratios in French wheat. In barley, exports increased by 2 million metric tons, from approximately 2.8 million metric tons in 1983–84 to 4.8 million in 1984–85. About 8 percent of this increase was due to the development of sales to non-EC countries, primarily to the Soviet Union and Saudi Arabia. The report concluded that these results secured France's position as the number one grain producer and exporter in the European Community.

But French markets had come under American pressure as the world wheat market became depressed in late 1985. The volume of trade was low, and the demand for grain suffered from improved harvests in traditional grain-importing zones—North Africa and especially the USSR. Coincidental with this decline, grain prices were lower in 1985 than in 1984. The price of wheat, for example, varied between $140 and $145 per metric ton in 1984, whereas it dropped to around $115 per metric ton in 1985.

The sharp decline in world prices was accelerated by the May announcement of the U.S. Export Enhancement Program. After weeks of hesitation, on September 13, 1985, the USDA concluded its first EEP initiative, which involved 175,000 metric tons of wheat flour to Egypt. An additional EEP initiative for 500,000 metric tons of wheat to Egypt was concluded shortly thereafter. The French report estimated that the United States sold the wheat at between $15 and $20 per metric ton below the world price. The report concluded that because of the EEP, it was unlikely that wheat prices in the near future could go beyond $105 per metric ton.

The French grain harvest of 1985–86 had declined in quality because of excess humidity, and the volume of wheat had decreased to 5 million metric tons. Nevertheless, the French government believed it was necessary to maintain existing efforts to export in world markets. The report pointed out that France had accumulated stocks of 10 million metric tons of wheat and between 2 and 3 million metric tons of barley. It warned that if France did not maintain its present level of grain exports, surplus production would soon become so great as to become unbearable.

The report argued for French wheat exports to Europe at least as great as the previous year (that is, 6 million metric tons) or greater (7–7.5 million metric tons) on the strength of the poor quality of wheat harvests in neighboring European countries. For countries outside of the EC, French exports might increase from 7 million metric tons to 10 million, depending on the reaction of these countries to the level of French wheat subsidies made in the face of the "American offensive on our markets." The competition for subsidized wheat exports should be spread among Eastern bloc countries, presumably including the USSR (5–7 million metric tons); North Africa (2 million metric tons); and the rest of the world.

Competition for Grain Markets

As of September 30, 1985, the USDA had announced six EEP initiatives (Table 4.1), but only the one—to Egypt for wheat flour—had been successfully concluded. Critics declared the program a failure. They were not, however, evaluating the program in terms of the administration's overriding policy objective of increasing the costs to the European Community of subsidizing grain exports. By that standard, the impact of the Export Enhancement Program on the European Community was almost immediate. A pattern soon emerged. The European Community aggressively sought markets in Africa and North Yemen.

[69]

Table 4.1. EEP initiatives through September 1985

Target country	Date announced	Commodity by volume
Algeria	June 4	1 MT wheat
Egypt	July 2	600,000 MT wheat flour
Egypt	July 26	500,000 MT wheat
Yemen Arab Republic	August 20	50,000 MT wheat flour
Yemen Arab Republic	September 6	100,000 MT wheat
Morocco	September 30	1.5 MT wheat

Source: U.S. House of Representatives, Committee on Agriculture, *Review of the Export Enhancement Program Announced by the U.S. Department of Agriculture*, 99th Cong., 1st sess., serial 9916, 1985:69.

In September 1985, for example, the USDA offered to sell Egypt 250,000 metric tons of wheat at $109.95 each. That offer included a subsidy of about $21, or $2.94 per bushel. In response, the EC simply increased its subsidy to $42.00 dollars a metric ton. Not surprisingly, the EC beat the U.S. offer and made the sale. The EC also outbid the EEP offer to supply wheat flour to Yemen in 1985. The community offered to sell wheat flour at $174 a metric ton, which was about $3 below the U.S. offer. It established a line of credit to Morocco of $500,000 and sold Morocco 110,000 metric tons of wheat at prices between $104.00 and $105.75 per ton. With U.S. soft wheat prices at the Gulf price[1] of about $115.00 per ton, the EC wheat sale to Morocco represented a subsidy of more than $10.00 per ton, or a total of $1.1 million.

In the cases of Algeria, Morocco, and North Yemen, the initial EEP bids were unsuccessful for the same reason. The EC simply increased its export subsidies to make European wheat more price competitive than U.S. wheat under the Export Enhancement Program. Critics accused the administration of failing to make a greater effort to beat the EC competition in North African

[1]The Gulf price of U.S. wheat is the cash market price at New Orleans, Louisiana. It includes the cost of transportation, elevating the grain from wholesalers, cleaning the barges that carry the grain from the point of origination to the port of export, and federal grain inspections.

markets, but the administration had at least succeeded in making these sales costly ones for the European Community. In the sales to Morocco and Algeria, for example, the EC had to offer wheat with a $70 per metric ton (or $1.91 per bushel) export subsidy, effectively lowering the price of wheat to these North African countries to $102 per metric ton (or $2.78 per bushel).

After September 1985, the United States was more successful in completing its EEP initiatives, but the EC continued to counter the U.S. initiatives with increases in export subsidies to try to retain its markets, as predicted by the administration. Figure 4.1 shows the mean monthly subsidy of EEP initiatives and the maximum EC export refunds for wheat in U.S. dollars from 1985 to 1988. The graph is based on the data presented in Table 4.2, which gives the mean monthly value of all export bids accepted by the CCC under the EEP and the maximum EC export refunds for this period. Critics argue that while the Export Enhancement Program did indeed increase the cost to the EC of subsidizing its exports, the same result could have been achieved by simply releasing U.S. grain stocks into the world market, depressing world market prices and thereby increasing EC subsidies. This criticism once again misses the point of the policy: The EEP was targeted to increase the budgetary pressure on the European Community incrementally, whereas a blanket release of surplus grain stocks would have had unpredictable consequences for all grain exporting countries, including the United States.

EC export refunds are usually announced for particular commodities and seven geographic zones, each of which is comprised of several countries. In exceptional circumstances, however, the EC has announced special export refunds for specific countries. Before the EEP was introduced, the variation in export refunds between zones was largely due to the differences in the cost of transporting commodities to importing countries. After the Export Enhancement Program was inaugurated, however, variations also reflected the targeting of exports to specific countries to compete with U.S. exports (*C.A.P. Monitor*, 1987: 10–19, 20).

Figure 4.1 shows that the EC's maximum export refunds for common wheat for the period from 1985 through 1988 were

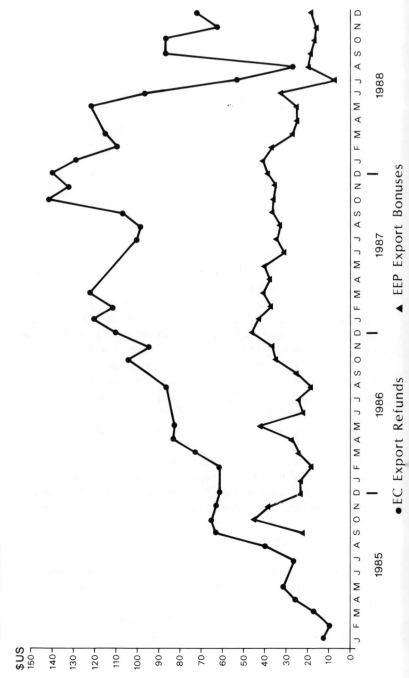

Figure 4.1. U.S. and EC wheat export subsidies. From Home-Grown Cereals Authority of London, *Weekly Bulletin*; and Foreign Agricultural Service of the USDA.

Table 4.2. EEP and EC wheat export subsidies (monthly mean values in U.S. dollars per metric ton)

	1985		1986		1987		1988	
	EEP	EC[a]	EEP	EC[a]	EEP	EC[a]	EEP	EC[a]
Jan.		11.65	23.07	—[b]	42.89	120.25	40.84	128.45
Feb.		9.46	18.43	61.16	36.58	111.13	36.74	109.27
Mar.		16.24	24.45	73.18	41.09	121.99	27.00	113.31
Apr.		26.43	26.56	82.68	37.77	—[b]	25.34	118.28
May		30.80	41.72	81.97	40.28	—[b]	24.75	121.06
June		—[b]	21.51	—[b]	30.58	—[b]	33.32	96.95
July		25.68	23.72	—[b]	34.30	99.92	7.34	53.47
Aug.		38.73	18.34	86.09	32.85	98.78	20.29	27.34
Sept.	21.83	63.09	25.22	95.17	37.24	106.74	18.56	86.72
Oct.	45.28	64.59	35.11	104.39	36.17	141.17	16.65	86.75
Nov.	38.32	62.80	36.10	94.31	34.91	131.98	15.63	61.94
Dec.	23.13	60.56	45.78	109.58	39.05	139.78	17.98	71.90

Source: Home-Grown Cereals Authority of London, *Weekly Bulletins* and HGCA work sheets of EEC weekly export tenders by commodity, 1985–89; and Foreign Agricultural Service of the USDA, program announcements of export enhancement bid acceptances, 1985–89.

[a]Based on maximum export refunds in EC weekly tenders.
[b]Export refunds not awarded.

highly sensitive to the export bonuses in the EEP initiatives. For example, in response to the completion of the first EEP initiative in September 1985, the EC's export subsidy almost doubled, from $38.75 per metric ton in August to $63.09 in September. In every month from mid-1985 through 1988, the EC's export subsidies were significantly higher than U.S. subsidies. In April 1986, for example, the EC subsidy was $82.68 while the U.S. subsidy was only $26.56; in January 1987, it rose to $120.25 while the American subsidy was $42.89; and in December 1987, the EC subsidy rose to its highest point, at $139.78, while the U.S. subsidy remained at a relatively low $39.05—a difference of almost $100 more per metric ton of wheat.

The only change in this trend occurred from June through August 1988, during the severe drought in the major grain-growing areas of the United States. The effect of the drought was to raise speculation among traders and producers about a major shortfall in the forthcoming U.S. wheat harvest. This speculation provoked a substantial rise in the world price of wheat, enabling the EC to reduce its export subsidies, which are a function of the difference between the EC market price and the world price (that is, the U.S. Gulf price). In recognition of this fact, the United States also lowered its export subsidies. The EC's wheat subsidy remained, however, substantially above the U.S. subsidy even during the drought.

This episode suggests that the United States strategically lowered its wheat subsidies during the period of high world prices for cereals because it recognized that U.S. subsidies did not have the same adverse budgetary impact on the EC at such times. That U.S. subsidies were geared more to pressuring the EC than to domestic considerations is evident in the U.S. decision to increase export subsidies soon after the world price for wheat dropped in September 1988, while the drought in the United States continued. The U.S. subsidy increased from $7.34 in July to $18.56 in September, while the EC subsidy increased by a substantially larger margin—from $27.34 in August to $86.75 in October. The subsidies continued to fluctuate in relation to one another during early 1989, with EC export subsidies substantially higher. For example, in January and February the EEP subsidy for wheat export was $18.11 and $13.76 respectively while the EC subsidy for these months was $67.39 and $43.24.

The Home-Grown Cereals Authority (HGCA) of London also produced a graph comparing the EEP bonus rates granted for hard red winter wheat with the EC export refund rates for French milling wheat for all sales, from the first ones under the Export Enhancement Program in 1985 through the end of 1988 (HGCA *Weekly Digest*, February 13, 1989). The subsidy profiles generally correspond to those in Figure 4.1. The total average U.S. bonus over the period was $31.59 per metric ton compared with the EC average of $114.10 per metric ton (HGCA *Weekly Digest*, February 6, 1989).

A similar pattern of U.S.-EC export subsidies obtained for barley, the second-largest Export Enhancement Program commodity by volume (Table 4.3). The data in Table 4.3 is plotted in Figure 4.2, which shows that the EC's export refunds for barley were substantially higher beginning in June 1986, when the first EEP initiative was concluded, and continuing through 1988. For

Table 4.3. EEP and EC barley export subsidies (monthly mean values in U.S. dollars per metric ton)

	1985	1986		1987		1988	
	EC[a]	EEP	EC[a]	EEP	EC[a]	EEP	EC[a]
Jan.	25.50		81.13	41.90	123.82	42.27	136.03
Feb.	23.99		88.58	42.79	122.02	38.94	121.37
Mar.	29.90		98.88	40.28	127.77	39.47	119.03
Apr.	42.48		117.98	—[b]	133.01	29.48	121.62
May	49.73		119.75	46.71	136.11	21.40	119.31
June	—[b]	37.93	—[b]	39.08	—[b]	21.78	83.32
July	44.30	31.84	85.67	33.28	99.10	—[b]	67.96
Aug.	52.81	28.06	95.91	43.54	96.98	—[b]	39.62
Sept.	63.22	30.95	109.90	44.59	107.73	—[b]	65.44
Oct.	72.01	35.98	105.62	—[b]	126.19	—[b]	72.82
Nov.	74.50	46.35	—[b]	54.33	134.57	3.88	—[b]
Dec.	74.55	—[b]	—[b]	50.40	141.81	13.20	82.61

Source: Home-Grown Cereals Authority of London, *Weekly Bulletins* and HGCA work sheets of EC weekly export tenders by commodity, 1985–89; and Foreign Agricultural Service of the USDA, program announcements of export enhancement bid acceptances, 1985–89.

[a]Based on maximum export refunds in EC weekly tenders.

[b]Export refunds not awarded.

example, in October 1986 the EEP subsidy was $35.98 per metric ton while the EC subsidy was $105.62, and in December 1987, the respective subsidies were $50.40 and $141.81.

Like wheat export subsidies, barley subsidies dropped (in this case, from June through December of 1988) in response to the rise in world prices, and like wheat export subsidies, EC barley subsidies remained significantly higher than U.S. subsidies during the period of lower prices. In May, before the U.S. drought had an effect on world market prices, the U.S. subsidy stood at $21.40; by August it had dropped to nil. In contrast, the EC barley subsidy declined from $119.31 in May to $39.62 in August. The same pattern obtained in early 1989. In January the EEP subsidy was nil and in February it was $16.72, while the EC subsidies for these months were $78.30 and $79.02 respectively. These data suggest that the EC's export subsidies are extremely sensitive to EEP initiatives and that the EC is determined to

Figure 4.2. U.S. and EC barley export subsidies. From Home-Grown Cereals Authority of London, *Weekly Bulletin*; and Foreign Agricultural Service of the USDA.

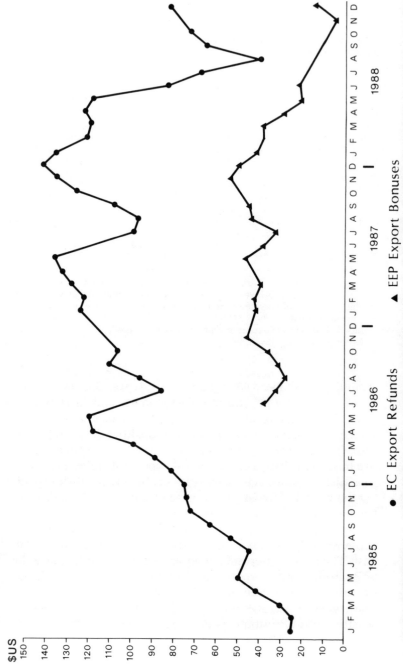

outbid U.S. agricultural export initiatives to retain and expand export markets in cereals.

Evaluating the Export Enhancement Program

The two principal objectives for the Export Enhancement Program were to restore U.S. grain markets lost to EC countries through "unfair" subsidized competition and to punish these countries by making it prohibitively expensive for them to engage in a subsidy war with the United States. The program was intended to be short term, so it is appropriate to evaluate its performance after three or four years of operation.

Restoring U.S. Markets

During congressional hearings in 1988 before a subcommittee of the Committee on Appropriations of the House of Representatives, an administration spokesman claimed that the EEP had restored U.S. dominance in world grain markets. Thomas Kay, the FAS administrator, testified that 1988 would be a "banner year" for U.S. agricultural exports. Exports, he said, should increase in value by 16 percent over 1987, to $32.5 billion in fiscal year 1988, and in volume by one-tenth, to 142.5 million metric tons, matching the high annual increases of the 1970s. As a result, the U.S. agricultural trade surplus would, he expected, reach $12 billion, a $5 billion increase over the 1987 figure of $7 billion. Kay argued that market penetration was "one of the most effective things about EEP," particularly with reference to wheat exports (U.S. House of Representatives, 1988:616).

The United States was able to restore lost markets by increasing its share of wheat and wheat flour exports in world markets from a low of 30.9 percent in 1985 to 38.9 percent in 1988 (Table 4.4). This increase resulted from exporting at least 42 million metric tons of wheat in 1988, which was more wheat than the United States had shipped out of the country in any year since 1964. According to USDA, the value of U.S. wheat and flour exports went from $6.7 billion in fiscal year 1984 to $4.4 billion

Protecting Markets

Table 4.4. The United States' and its competitors' wheat
and wheat flour trade (in million metric tons)

	U.S.	Competitors	U.S. market position (%)
1987–88	39.5	52.6	38.9
1986–87	30.1	57.2	32.1
1985–86	27.1	53.5	31.5
1984–85	29.6	58.5	30.9
1983–84	43.4	59.2	40.0
1982–83	39.4	54.0	39.6
1981–82	45.8	48.7	46.5
1980–81	43.7	44.4	46.4
1979–80	38.3	44.2	44.4
1978–79	38.3	44.2	42.6
1977–78	33.6	30.9	67.2

Source: U.S. House of Representatives, *Rural Development, Agriculture and Related Agencies Appropriations for 1989: Excerpts from Hearings*, pt. 4, 100th Cong., 2d sess., March 1988:643.

in 1985, $3.5 billion in 1986, $3.1 billion in 1987 and was forecast to earn $4.1 billion in 1988 (U.S. House of Representatives, 1988:711).

Kay said that the U.S. had restored its market dominance in the Soviet Union, China, and North Africa. The USSR, for example, bought 6.8 million metric tons of wheat from the United States in 1988, which brought them "back into our market." He credited the program with sales of 5.2 million metric tons of wheat to China in 1987 and described it as redeeming U.S. grain markets in North Africa (Morocco, Algeria, Tunisia, Libya, and Egypt) which the "EC took away." Kay claimed that the EEP enabled the United States to capture the poultry market in the Canary Islands, which subsequently purchased American poultry on a commercial basis. He also said the program expanded U.S. exports of barley and processed products.

Figure 4.3, which compares U.S. and EC subsidized wheat prices from October 1985 through December 1988, shows a strong correlation between U.S. and EC subsidized wheat prices, reflecting an intense competition for markets. EC subsidized wheat exports were competitive with U.S. exports during the

Figure 4.3. Comparison of U.S. and EC subsidized wheat prices (October 1985–December 1988). From Home-Grown Cereals Authority of London, *Weekly Bulletin*, February 13, 1989.

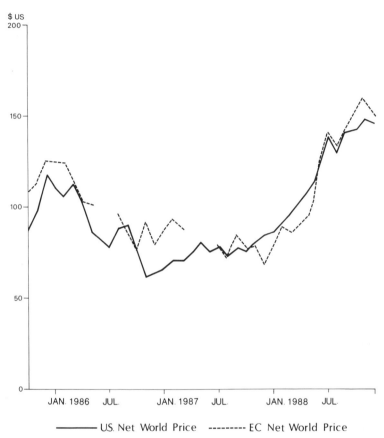

1987–88 season, but from the beginning of the 1988–89 season, U.S. subsidized prices tended to undercut the net EC price. The result was a heavy volume of U.S. sales under the Export Enhancement Program, including the sale of 12.5 million metric tons of wheat to the USSR and 17.2 million metric tons to China between May 1988 and October 1991.

Although it is clear that the Export Enhancement Program

Table 4.5. French and EC exports of wheat to non-EC countries (in thousand metric tons)

	1986	1987
French exports to:		
USSR	3,279	3,000
Poland	191	236
Algeria	127	260
Tunisia	409	328
Ivory Coast	218	249
Syria	401	271
China	94	408
Bangladesh	84	263
Brazil	—	617
Nigeria	105	—
South Korea	—	70
Ethiopia	42	—
Canary Islands	—	102
Total	5,930	7,232
EC exports	9,202	11,853

Source: Home-Grown Cereals Authority, supplement to *Weekly Bulletin,* January 16, 1989.

stimulated an expansion of U.S. grain exports, it does not necessarily follow that, in doing so, the United States had taken markets away from the EC. That can be ascertained by examining the pattern of European Community wheat exported to non-EC countries after 1985. Table 4.5, with its data on French and EC wheat exports to major non-EC clients for 1986 and 1987, shows that French exports of wheat to the USSR, China, and North Africa did not decline overall. The export of EC wheat flour, barley, and malt to non-EC countries follows a similar pattern, with France exporting 50 percent or more of total EC exports. The quantity of EC wheat exported to the USSR in 1986 was 5.0 million metric tons; in 1987 it was 5.2 million.

The French National Cereals Office reported French cereal export statistics for the first five months of the 1988 season, up to December 1988 (HGCA *Weekly Digest,* January 30, 1989). French cereal growers harvested a bumper crop of 54.8 million metric tons of grain. Soft wheat production was 28.5 million metric tons, the highest yield since 1984. At the same time, Soviet grain production dropped to its lowest yield in three years, necessitating Soviet imports as high as 40 million metric tons. The Soviet grain deficit, along with the dangerously low level of U.S. grain stocks after the drought, created a significant export potential for French cereals.[2] French wheat exports up to December 1, 1988, totaled 5.5 million metric tons, a slight increase over the previous season, but wheat exports to non-EC destinations increased by 22 percent. Barley exports were 18 percent higher because of significantly increased exports to non-EC countries, particularly Algeria. French wheat exports for the 1989–90 season were just over 6 million metric tons and were projected to rise to 9 million metric tons in 1991–92.

It is clear, therefore, that while the EEP has increased U.S. grain exports, it has not taken markets away from the EC. The USDA has estimated, for example, that the EC exported a record 21 million metric tons of wheat during the 1988–89 marketing year (U.S. Department of Agriculture, 1989:2, 19). One reason the EEP is unlikely to displace the EC from grain markets is that the price of cereals is not the only, nor even the most important, consideration for many major grain-buying countries. In North Africa, for example, credit availability and food security are more important than price. In Algeria and Egypt, which both need to import more than 60 percent of their wheat and flour requirements, a policy of diversified supplies is followed, to avoid dependence on a single source. In Morocco, the critical factor is buying from the country that offers the best credit terms.

Putting Pressure on the EC Budget

To say that EC export refunds are higher than EEP bonuses because the European Community has substantially higher sup-

---

[2] Wheat stocks in the United States declined from 51.8 million metric tons in the 1985–86 marketing year to only 14.9 million in the 1988–89 marketing year (U.S. Department of Agriculture, 1989:23).

port prices for cereals than the United States does is deceptive; for it is to ignore hidden U.S. subsidies in the form of deficiency payments paid to American farmers. These are direct payments, made by the USDA, to make up the difference between the low prices farmers might receive for their products on the U.S. market and the politically determined higher guaranteed minimum, or target prices, set to ensure a minimum income for farm households.

Deficiency payments go to farmers who participate in feed grain, wheat, rice, or cotton programs. From the 1920s to 1960 these payments constituted a relatively small part of farmers' income—rarely as much as 10 percent of the average farm family's net cash income. By the 1980s, however, the federal government had become a major source of farm income. In 1987, for example, net farm income reached a high of $57 billion, of which the government contributed 30 percent, or $17 billion, in direct payments. During President Reagan's second term, agriculture became the fastest-growing item in the federal budget. In 1986, the farm program was the third-largest benefit program after Social Security and Medicare.

What is politically significant about the fact that the EC's export refunds are larger than EEP bonuses is not the relative size of government subsidies. Since 1982, U.S. and EC governmental expenditures on agricultural support programs have actually been roughly comparable. Table 4.6 shows that from 1982 through 1987, U.S. expenditure on agricultural support varied from 50.3 to 134.4 percent of EC expenditure. In 1987, U.S. expenditure was 83.6 percent of total EC governmental outlay.

Rather, it is the significant fact that the EC must finance its CAP program, including export refunds, out of its own resources. Unlike the United States, the EC cannot run deficits to finance its operations. Budget increases must receive the approval of member governments, so any expansion of export refunds that increases the budget must receive the endorsement of all member states including the United Kingdom. Roberts (of the Australian Bureau of Agricultural and Resource Economics, private communication, October 19, 1990) compares the EC budget to a soufflé with a lid on it: if the pressure becomes too

Table 4.6. U.S. and EC government expenditure on agricultural support (in billions of U.S. dollars)

	United States (A)	EC-10[a] (B)	(A) as % of (B)
1990[b]	6.7	34.2	19.6
1989	10.5	28.5	36.8
1988	12.5	32.7	38.2
1987	22.4	26.8	83.6
1986	25.8	21.8	118.3
1985	17.6	15.1	116.6
1984	7.3	14.5	50.3
1983	18.8	14.2	134.4
1982	11.6	12.2	95.1
1981	4.0	12.5	32.0
1980	2.7	15.7	17.2
1979	3.6	14.3	25.2
1978	5.6	11.1	50.1
1977	3.8	8.0	47.5

Source: USDA, Economic Research Service, *Western Europe Agriculture and Trade Report*, 1990.

[a]In 1985 the European Community consisted of ten members (EC-10): Belgium, Federal Republic of Germany, France, Italy, Luxembourg, the Netherlands, Denmark, Ireland, the United Kingdom, and Greece. In 1986, two more countries were admitted—Portugal and Spain—bringing the total to twelve (EC-12)

[b]Preliminary.

great, the European Council of Ministers will eventually agree to a rise. While historically this has been the case, there have been, and continue to be, major political disputes over raising budget limits. Furthermore, pressure builds in the EC to reform the CAP precisely because of the limits placed on the EC budget.

The European Agricultural Guidance and Guarantee Fund absorbs roughly 70 percent of the total EC budget expenditure. Its guarantee section uses the lion's share, about 68 percent of the EAGGF budget, to finance export refunds, making them the largest item in the CAP budget. Table 4.7 traces the EAGGF expenditure from 1983 through 1988. It shows a substantial increase in EAGGF guarantee expenditure, from 15,811.6 million ECUs in 1983 to 27,687.3 million in 1988 (over which time, EC member-

Protecting Markets

Table 4.7. EAGGF expenditure (in millions of ECUs)

	1983	1984	1985	1986	1987	198⬚
EAGGF guarantee	15,811.6	18,346.5	19,744.2	22,137.4	22,967.7	27,68⬚
EAGGF guidance	728.0	676.2	719.6	773.5	938.0	1,18⬚
Total gross expenditure	16,539.6	19,022.7	20,463.8	·22,910.9	23,905.7	28,86⬚
Ordinary levies	1,347.1	1,259.9	1,121.7	1,175.5	1,626.1	1,50⬚
Sugar levies	948.0	1,176.4	1,057.4	1,111.5	1,471.7	1,39⬚
Total net expenditures	14,244.5	16,586.4	18,284.7	20,623.9	20,807.9	25,97⬚

Source: Commission of the European Communities, *The Agricultural Situation in the Commr nity: 1987 Report* (Brussels: CEC, 1988), 95; and Commission of the European Communities, *T Agricultural Situation in the Community: 1990 Report* (Brussels: CEC, 1991), T84–85.

Table 4.8. EC budget and EAGGF expenditure (in millions of ECUs)

	1983	1984	1985	1986	1987	198⬚
EC budget	24,807.6	27,208.8	28,085.1	35,174.1	35,469.2	41,12⬚
EAGGF guarantee	14,224.4	16,586.4	18,284.7	20,623.9	22,967.7	27,68⬚
EAGGF as % of budget	57	61	65	59	65	6⬚

Source: Commission of the European Communities, The Agricultural Situation in the Commr nity: 1987 Report (Brussels: CEC, 1988), 95, T83; and Commission of the European Communiti⬚ *The Agricultural Situation in the Community: 1990 Report* (Brussels: CEC, 1991), T84.

ship increased from ten to twelve countries). Table 4.8 shows EAGGF guarantee expenditure as a percentage of total EC budget. The EAGGF guarantee expenditure constituted well over 50 percent of the total EC budget, rising to 67 percent of the total in 1988. The data also show that both the EC budget and the EAGGF guarantee expenditure increased by over 50 percent from 1983 through 1988.

EC export refunds for cereals make up the single largest expenditure item of the EAGGF budget. In 1988, cereal refunds amounted to 3,083.0 million ECUs out of a total EAGGF guarantee expenditure of 28,518.5 million ECUs. Furthermore, cereal refunds increased significantly after 1984: from 1,076.7 million ECUs (or 5.4 percent of the EAGGF guarantee expenditure in 1985) to 1988's figure of 3,083.0 million ECUs, which was 11 percent of the total (Commission of the European Communities, 1991:T85, T87). The size of cereal refunds and the rapid rate at which they grew made those refunds a sensitive political issue in the EC's annual budget debates. The Export Enhancement Program's impact on the EC's cereal refunds did, therefore, give the United States political leverage over the European Community's agricultural export policy.

Chapter Five

The Political Context of
the American Trade Assault

The political significance of the Export Enhancement Program as an instrument of U.S. foreign policy can only be determined in the context of EC politics. There is no doubt that, from the inception of the program in 1985 until the U.S. drought in 1988, the EEP increased the EC's costs of exporting grain outside the community.[1] This in itself was not, however, the objective. Rather, the aim was to increase EC *political* costs in order to persuade the EC to discontinue its "trade distorting" export subsidy policy. The true measure of success, then, is the exacerbation of existing political tension within the EC.

Until the world price of grain increased because of the U.S. drought and the rising value of the U.S. dollar, the Export Enhancement Program clearly did increase EC political tensions, enough, in fact, to threaten the viability of the institution itself. The tension was primarily between the United Kingdom and France, with Germany aligning itself with France in the interest of guaranteeing a minimum income for its farmers. Prime Minister Thatcher refused to agree to an increase in the Common

---

[1]Estimates of those costs vary, however, from as low as 2 percent to as high as 30 percent of the CAP budget, depending on the assumptions and the period covered (U.S. General Accounting Office, 1989:8).

Agricultural Policy budget until there was an agreement to limit agricultural spending programs. France and Germany took the position that revenues for CAP should be increased to meet current expenditures and only then should reductions be made in agricultural programs. Lacking evidence of real interest in reducing the EC's agricultural expenditures, the British remained skeptical and stood firm. The EEP came to play a key role in the controversy. At the February 1988 summit meeting of the European heads of government, cereal support costs became the principal political issue, leading to a stalemate between the British government, on the one hand, and the French and German governments on the other.

This alignment has a history in EC relations. The Germans have tended to support the French resistance to any reduction in CAP spending. Going back to 1981, Chancellor Helmut Schmidt's profarmer Free Democratic party agriculture minister Josef Ertl stressed his government's opposition to any "dilution of CAP." Speaking during Green Week in Berlin in January, he argued that any weakening of CAP or its principles would be the beginning of the end for the EC. Rather, the CAP should be strengthened to ensure the creation of food "reserves" so that the EC could fulfill its obligations to the Third World and to neighboring countries such as Poland. He did concede, however, that a strong CAP did not mean carte blanche for the production of food surpluses for which there was no need (*Agra Europe*, January 23, 1981:P/4).

The French government also strongly endorsed the CAP in 1981. Edith Cresson, François Mitterrand's Socialist minister of agriculture, elaborated the new government's position on the EC's agricultural policy in a statement issued in June: the "CAP's principles" should be "strengthened" before any spending restrictions were placed on the CAP. She argued that EC food surpluses were an important contribution to the world food supply and stressed that the only real common policy the EC had was the CAP. The EC's budget problems could not, she asserted, be resolved by limiting agricultural expenditure.

Cresson also set forth an anti-American theme that is a major feature of French Socialist thinking: that the United States should not have a monopoly on world food trade. In response to U.S. agriculture secretary John Block's criticism of EC agricultural protectionism, Cresson said that the United States should not feed the whole world with its farm exports. She specifically challenged U.S. policy by stating that France would enter into negotiations with the USSR on grain sales despite the American trade embargo against the Soviet Union imposed by President Jimmy Carter. The U.S. grain embargo had, she said, demonstrated to the USSR that it was in its interests to diversify its sources of grain imports to be less dependent on the United States. France would seek to exploit this opportunity to expand its agricultural exports (*Agra Europe*, June 12, 1981:P/7).

Michael Rocard, the French minister for agriculture in 1983, reaffirmed Cresson's position. Given the dilemma of surplus agricultural production and the depletion of the EC's financial resources, the community was faced with two choices as he saw it: to pursue a strong export-oriented policy or to administer a no-growth CAP. Rocard strongly favored the first (*Le Monde*, May 18, 1983:1).

Firm British opposition goes back to 1979, when Margaret Thatcher took office. She soon launched a political campaign designed to reduce Britain's contribution to the EC budget. At the Dublin summit in November, she elaborated the British complaint. In 1970, during negotiations for British entry into the EC, her government was given assurances that if an "unacceptable situation" arose over its budget contributions, corrective action would be taken (*Times of London*, November 30, 1979:1). The prime minister said that Britain's receipts per head were only one-half the community average and that if receipts were raised to near the average, Britain's net contribution of just over £1,000 million would be cut to about £350 million.[2] Thatcher also stated that she favored reducing agricultural expenditure, which consumed approximately 75 percent of the entire EC budget, and increasing nonagricultural spending without increasing the overall budget. The reaction was predictably hos-

[2]Simply put: if Britain's total receipts from the EC's budget were higher, then its net contribution to the community budget would be lower.

tile. The Belgian foreign minister, Henri Simonet, spoke for the eight other EC member states: "If one country wants to pay less, other countries must pay more," and the most the other governments would offer Thatcher was a budget refund of about £350 million in 1980 and comparable refunds for the next two or three years.

At the Brussels summit the next year, the French stated that unless Britain agreed to a generous increase in farm prices, there could be no settlement of Britain's budget dispute with the EC, thus crystallizing out the dilemma that has been at the center of EC political controversy ever since. On the one hand, there is the demand of 11 million EC farmers for increases in the CAP guarantees of minimum prices for their products to compensate for the decline in their real income. On the other hand, with the EC self-sufficient in food production and generating surpluses, there is an urgent need to prevent agricultural expenditure from growing faster than total budget revenue. Britain, as a major net contributor, was in the position to simply refuse to increase its contribution to the budget.

The Farm Price Controversy

The EC budget controversy centers on the community's annual price fixing to guarantee farmers a minimum income. The prices are supposed to equal the minimum return that will yield a reasonable standard of living. The Comité des Organisations Professionnelles Agricoles de la Communauté Européenne (COPA, Committee of Agricultural Organizations in the European Community) has argued that any problem caused by increased EAGGF expenditures should be resolved by simply increasing the EC's own resources rather than by placing limitations on CAP spending. COPA has advocated higher levels of EC funding to increase farmers' income and takes the position that the surplus production problem has been exaggerated and could easily be resolved through subsidized sales and an aggressive food export policy.

The French and German governments have tended to support

COPA's demand for higher prices, usually in response to national farmer protests. In February of 1981, for example, German farmers mounted their largest demonstration since the end of World War II. More than one hundred thousand farmers took to the streets in 150 cities and towns to protest the German government's and the EC's policies. The protest was triggered by frustration over Chancellor Schmidt's failure to support higher farm prices to reverse a decline in farm income. Constantin von Heeremann, president of the farmers' association, said that farmers' income had declined by 25 percent since 1975 (*Times of London*, February 16, 1981:4).

The French government is haunted by the fear of farmers rioting in the streets, especially right before presidential elections, as in April 1981, when thousands of French farmers threw stones and bottles and engaged in street battles in Brussels, demanding a 15 percent price increase (*Le Monde*, April 1, 1981:1). Under pressure, the EC agricultural ministers reached agreement on a 9.5 percent average increase in minimum prices guaranteed to farmers in 1981. When this increase was added to the "green" currency devaluations (rates at which the ECU is converted into national currencies for farm policy purposes), the prices paid to French farmers actually increased an additional 2.5 percent, bringing the overall increase close to the 15 percent farmers demanded.[3] While the British grudgingly agreed to the price increase, they continued to attack the CAP for swallowing too large a share of the European Community's funds and stimulating surplus food production.

[3]"Green" currency is a mechanism for applying a special exchange rate to farm products without a corresponding upward reevaluation of other commodities. Its purpose is to protect farmers against currency changes. For example, in 1984 the Commission of the European Communities recommended that the green pound rate be readjusted to take into account Britain's low rate of inflation. If the commission's recommendation had been accepted, it would have meant that British farmers' sterling income from the CAP would have declined on average by 3.2 percent. In contrast, the relatively high rate of inflation in France would have meant an upward revision of the green franc rate by the same 3.2 percent, meaning French farmers would have received a 3.2 percent increase in prices for their products (*Times of London*, January 13, 1984:6).

Since 1981, positions have remained unchanged. The British have called for farm price restraint, suggesting annual increases between 4 and 5 percent or lower. As Sir Geoffrey Howe, the chancellor of the exchequer, pointed out, when appealing for restraint, farmers were not the only ones to have suffered a loss of income (*Times of London*, February 17, 1981:5). Most other EC governments have sought double-digit price increases to satisfy the powerful farm lobby. The Commission of the European Communities has tried to work out a compromise between the two positions, and inevitably, the prices have risen and, along with them, the agricultural share of the EC budget.

At a meeting of the EC agricultural ministers in Brussels in March 1981, the French leader, Jacques Chirac, attacked the British for refusing to agree to higher farm prices, accusing them of obstinacy and hypocrisy. He said that if the British were not prepared to go along with the EC's decisions, then they should leave the European Community. The British countered with the assertion that it was better to subsidize food consumption inside the EC than to sell food surpluses outside the EC at subsidized prices—a comment directed at the French (*Times of London*, March 31, 1981:8). Rhetoric aside, the 1981 farm price settlement aggravated an already serious EC budgetary problem. The European Parliament (which must approve the Council of Minister's proposed EC budgets) voted for a 12 percent increase in farm prices, an increase significantly above the 7.8 percent the commission had recommended, yet below COPA's projected 15 percent necessary to keep pace with inflation. Christopher Tugendhat, the commissioner in charge of the budget, predicted that by 1982 the European Parliament's proposed increase would double the cost for which the commission had budgeted and farm support costs would rise above the rate of increase in EC revenues (*Times of London*, March 27, 1981:9).

Tough bargaining brought the increase down to 9.5 percent, still one of the highest price increases since Britain joined the EC. It was expected to increase the budgetary cost by at least one thousand million pounds. It would certainly not reduce agriculture's roughly 70 percent of total EC expenditure, meaning no funds would be made available for investment in Britain, which had a relatively small agricultural sector. Moreover, the price increase exceeded the forecasted rate of inflation for 1981; breaking the pattern set in previous years. After currency adjustments, the highest real price increases went to the countries with the greatest food surpluses—France, Netherlands, Denmark, and Germany.

During the 1982 price negotiations, Britain firmly opposed the EC commission's farm price proposal of a 9 percent increase. Peter Walker, the British minister of agriculture, said that the increase was not prudent and warned that agreement on the proposal would take as long as negotiations over Britain's contribution to the EC budget. But Britain stood alone. Other ministers said they would be happy to settle for a 9 percent increase, and France insisted on an increase of 14 percent (*Times of London*, March 16, 1982:6).

The French government was under intense political pressure from the seven hundred thousand–strong French National Farmers' Union. In March, François Guillaume, the union's leader, organized the biggest demonstration of farmers ever held in Paris (*Le Monde*, March 18, 1982:34). An estimated one hundred thousand farmers representing all commodities, agricultural regions, and sizes of enterprise converged on the Place de la Nation, demanding that the French government oppose the British and hold out for substantial increases in EC farm prices (*Times of London*, March 24, 1982:7).

The French response was predictably uncompromising. Agricultural Minister Cresson said that her government would not allow Britain to hold up farm price increases until agreement was reached on the United Kingdom's contribution to the EC budget; there would be no replay of 1980, when Britain had blocked a farm price increase until it had obtained a satisfactory refund of its net contribution to the EC budget (*Times of London*, March 17, 1982:6). In support of the French position, both farmers' organizations and the government quoted statistics released by the EC commission which showed that, since 1977, French farm incomes had declined more than those of any other EC country (Table 5.1). According to the commission report, lower French farm incomes date from 1973, three years before the decline in other EC countries. The cause was a combination

Table 5.1. Change in EC farmers' incomes, 1977–1981 (in percentages)

	Inflation[a]	National aids[a]	1981 income[b]
Italy	16.9 (9)	17.8	104.6 (1)
Ireland	14.7 (8)	16.6	104.0 (2)
Denmark	8.8 (5)	9.7	101.2 (3)
Netherlands	7.1 (3)	5.8	99.1 (4)
Belgium	7.1 (4)	6.4	98.3 (5)
Luxembourg	7.0 (2)	6.4	97.0 (6)
West Germany	4.9 (1)	5.0	94.7 (7)
United Kingdom	14.7 (7)	17.9	92.2 (8)
France	10.6 (6)	9.8	91.0 (9)

Source: Times of London, March 24, 1982:7.
Note: Figures in parentheses indicate rank.
[a]Annual average.
[b]100 percent is the average annual income for 1973–75.

of increased costs relative to prices and slower growth in agricultural production (*Times of London*, March 24, 1982:7).

Britain and Germany wanted to hold farm price increases to no more than 9 percent, while the French government continued to press for something closer to 14 percent. The European Parliament's agriculture committee was prepared to support farm price increases of 14 percent, while both the EC commission and Council of Ministers were committed to a lower figure. The European Parliament voted by a margin of 135 to 107 to recommend to the Council of Ministers a 14 percent increase in farm prices. This figure was, however, still below the 16.3 percent demanded by farmers' organizations such as COPA and the Comité Général de la Coopération Agricole des Pays de la CEE (COGECA, General Committee of Agricultural Cooperation in the EC).

The Isolation of Great Britain

The British government renewed its opposition to any agreement on EC farm price increases without a prior agreement to reduce the United Kingdom's net contribution to the EC budget. Peter Walker threatened to veto any deal on agricultural price rises until the budget conflict was settled. Britain and Germany were the only EC countries making net contributions to the community budget. Britain estimated that without concessions it would pay as much as one thousand million pounds in 1982, compared to only fifty-five million in 1981. The prime minister insisted on a five-year limit on Britain's net contribution. Its opponents countered that only after they knew the increased level of agricultural prices could they estimate the amount the British government would have to pay into the EC budget.

Britain's opponents received an unexpected boost when some British Conservative party members of the European Parliament opposed their prime minister. In May 1982, Sir Henry Plumb, a former president of the National Farmers' Union of Britain, with a small majority of the sixty-three Conservatives, opposed British minister for agriculture Walker in his efforts in the Council of Ministers to block a farm price settlement until a budget agreement had been reached. The British Conservatives took this action on the grounds that the so-called Luxembourg compromise of 1965 should no longer apply. The Luxembourg compromise was a principle established after France's six-month boycott of the Council of Ministers. To end the boycott, the council had agreed that on any issue where a member country's national interest was at stake, a unanimous vote in the Council of Ministers would be required. When the British Conservative party sponsored the passage of the European Communities Bill in 1972 for British admission to the EC, that right of national veto had served to reassure Britons opposed to EC membership.

When, therefore, the Conservatives supported a resolution of the European Parliament calling on the Council of Ministers to abandon the Luxembourg compromise and to approve the farm price settlement agreed to by all EC members except Britain, they were undercutting a hallowed principle of British membership (*Times of London*, May 14, 1982:4). Their break with the British government's position must be understood in part, at least, as reflecting a divergence of interests between British farmers and the government. The CAP had become a favorite whipping boy for all British political parties, but British farmers had come to realize that without it they would be faced with a reversion to the system of deficiency payments in place before Britain's entry into the EC. They were certain the Treasury would be reluctant to support a deficiency payment scheme that could cost as much as fifteen hundred million pounds annually. Such large-scale subsidies would be highly visible to the public, which would undoubtedly pressure the government to reduce them to substantially below EC-guaranteed CAP levels of farm support (*Times of London,* May 17, 1982:10).

On May 18, the Council of Ministers accepted, by majority vote, sixty-two regulations to increase farm prices despite British opposition. Seven members of the EC forced through a price package averaging an 11 percent increase, the effect of which was to boost agriculture's share of total EC spending from about 65 percent in 1981 to almost 70 percent in 1983. In taking this action, they ignored Britain's opposition. Britain did not formally exercise its veto power, and its negative vote on the package—on the grounds that it was inimical to its national interest—was brushed aside by EC colleagues. The British government condemned what it described as the destruction of the Luxembourg compromise. Not only had Britain's requested one-year budget rebate of £572 million been reduced to £452 million, but the United Kingdom would have to find an additional £112 million to pay for its share of the price increase.

In opposing the British position, the French argued that the veto could not be invoked in this particular instance because it was an agricultural and not a budgetary issue (*Le Monde,* May 19, 1982;1; *Times of London,* May 19, 1982:5). Walker called the French argument "a blatant absurdity." An unphased Mitterrand reiterated the French position that the EC had to face up to its responsibilities in regard to farm prices without delay. Because such increases were not retroactive, any delay meant a loss of revenue for farmers. Moreover, while France could accept the British demand for assistance to partners faced with an "intolerable" situation, it did not agree that Britain was entitled under the terms of the Treaty of Rome to an automatic and permanent reduction in its contribution to the community budget (*Times of London,* May 19, 1982:5).

The next year's farm price-fixing exercise in Luxembourg only confirmed Britain's isolation. As in previous years, the EC farm groups demanded at least a 7 percent average increase in farm prices. The farm lobby proved so influential that the European Parliament voted by 147 to 123 to approve the agriculture committee's recommendation to that effect (*Times of London*, March 11, 1983:6). The British Labour and Conservative members of the European Parliament who backed the British government's call for a freeze in farm prices were defeated. Walker argued that there should be no increase in prices for products already in surplus. He pointed out that nearly one-fourth of the EC's financial resources was being used in this way, depressing world markets and straining EC relations with the United States (*Times of London*, April 18, 1983:7), and that the EC Commission was in fact anxious to hold down farm price increases to demonstrate to the Reagan administration an eagerness to avoid a transatlantic agricultural trade dispute.

As always, the commission looked for a compromise. It proposed that average farm price increases be limited to 4.2 percent. The British argued that even that was too high; for it would add an additional £200 million to the EC budget in 1983 and a further £385 million in 1984, bringing the total close to the community's legal funding limit. It would also mean that agricultural spending was rising faster than the EC's ability to raise money. The Netherlands was prepared to accept the proposal. Germany was not prepared to state its position until after its general elections, scheduled for March 6—even though it held the presidency of the Council of Ministers and was therefore responsible for seeing that a satisfactory agreement was achieved. All other states favored increases in farm prices. France led the call for price increases at the level demanded by its farm organizations.

Farm Protest in France and Germany

The French and German positions were strongly influenced by their governments' concern about alienating voters in key farming areas. The French prime minister, Pierre Mauroy, was

forced to leave an agricultural exhibition when farmers pro-
tested his presence. They demanded that he resign and shouted
their support for Jacques Chirac, the leader of the right-wing
opposition Rally for the Republic party. The political significance of this protest was that it was the first one involving a
senior minister in President François Mitterrand's twenty-two
month–old government. The timing was also significant: it occurred shortly after Socialist party defeats in municipal elections. Mauroy enjoyed high public esteem early in the Mitterrand government and had defended the government in the
run-up to the municipal elections. Then, in late April, thousands of angry French farmers, unhappy that the delay in annual
farm price fixing was costing them millions in lost income,
chartered buses to travel to Luxembourg to pressure the EC
agriculture ministers (*Times of London*, April 28, 1983:6).

Ignaz Kiechle, the German agriculture minister and president
of the Council of Ministers, found himself in a dilemma. As
president of the council he was committed to keeping agricultural spending within existing limits. Yet if he supported the 4.2
percent average farm price increase recommended by the EC
Commission, the result would be a cut in the income of German
farmers, specifically, the Bavarian farmers who had elected him.
Therefore, instead of supporting his own commission's recommendations, Kiechle broke off farm price negotiations in the
council and returned to Bonn to seek permission to propose a
higher farm price increase (*Times of London*, April 20, 1983:6).

The Council of Ministers finally agreed to farm price increases
averaging just under 7 percent in the real currencies of member states but 4.2 percent in ECUs (Table 5.2). The price agreement represented a compromise primarily between Britain and
France. The EC Commission managed to persuade the Council of
Ministers that there was no point in raising farm prices beyond
the proposed 4.2 percent because the EC was already running
out of cash without the increase. Farm spending for the first
three months of 1983 was, after all, running at 30 percent above
the forecast, and any further increase could bankrupt the community. A supplementary budget was necessary just to meet the
extra costs.

Table 5.2. EC farm price increases,
1983 (in percentages)

West Germany	2.0
France	6.4
Italy	8.8
Netherlands	2.6
Belgium	4.4
Luxembourg	3.9
United Kingdom	4.1
Ireland	8.1
Denmark	4.0
Greece	14.0
EC average	5.5

Source: *Times of London*, May 18,
1983:11.
Note: Figures take into account green-
rate variations.

Attention then shifted temporarily from farm price increases
to fixing new exchange rates for the green currencies. Both the
French prime minister, who was now Michel Rocard, and British minister for agriculture Walker claimed a victory. According
to Rocard, he had won for the French farmers a "good agreement" that closed the gap between the weak "green franc" and
the strong "green mark," so that French food exports to West
Germany would increase. Germany had agreed to an upward
valuation of the deutsche mark by 5.5 percent. Walker took
credit for keeping farm price increases from getting out of hand
while securing a price rise for British farmers which would keep
them ahead of inflation in the United Kingdom.

The price settlement gave French farmers on average slightly
more than a 6 percent increase in the prices they received for
their commodities. Britain and Denmark would receive an increase of 4.2 percent on average. Germany and the Netherlands,
the countries with the strongest currencies in the community,
would have to accept an increase of only 2 and 2.6 percent
respectively; about 1 percent below the average in the EC. There
was a sense of relief in the community. Not only had the members avoided bankrupting the EC, but they also hoped this mod-
erate settlement would assuage American fears of an impending
agricultural trade war. The agricultural commissioner, Paul Dal-

Table 5.3. EC farm price increases, 1984 (in percentages)

	Price rise in national currencies	Rate of inflation
United Kingdom	−0.8	5.5
West Germany	−0.8	3.3
Netherlands	−0.5	3.7
Denmark	+1.5	5.3
Belgium	+2.7	6.5
Ireland	+2.7	9.0
Luxembourg	+2.8	7.7
France	+5.0	7.2
Italy	+6.4	10.8
Greece	+17.6	20.0
EC average	+3.2	5.2

Source: *Times of London*, April 2, 1984:6.

sager, said that the price settlement plus the modest price penalties imposed for cereal and dairy farmers would establish the EC's "good faith" with the Americans when talks with them resumed on how to avoid the all-out farm trade war the U.S. government had been threatening, should the EC fail to limit the growth of surplus production (*Economist*, May 21, 1983:72).

Complacency was not in order, however. At the next annual farm price-fixing settlement in April 1984, the EC adopted the most costly price increase in its history. The deal represented an average increase of 3.2 percent in real money terms throughout the community and was conservatively estimated to cost at least £544 million more than the price increase the previous year. After Greece and Italy, France received the highest price increase—5 percent—for its farmers. The United Kingdom, Germany, and the Netherlands, the countries with the strongest currencies, were net losers; their average prices declined by 0.5 percent or more (Table 5.3). None of the price increases even kept pace with the rate of inflation (Table 5.3), so despite the high cost of the settlement, EC farmers were not satisfied.

The leading force behind the price increase had been Rocard, who was anxious to placate the angry French farm lobby. Michael Jopling, then British minister of agriculture, had registered his government's displeasure with the settlement and insisted on placing in the minutes of the agreement Britain's desire to limit CAP spending for the year to the ten thousand million pounds already authorized in the EC budget—a clear signal that Britain would not contribute any additional funds to pay for extra costs arising from the higher price settlement (*Times of London,* April 2, 1984:6).

The 1985 EC deliberations on farm prices brought a major political impasse over cereals. The EC Commission's tough new agriculture commissioner, Frans Andriessen, put forth a farm price proposal that would have led to a virtual freeze in EC farm prices; for the net increase was to average only 0.1 percent. Based on this price package, the projected total cost to the EC would be a mere eighty million pounds, in stark contrast to a community budget bloated to roughly sixteen thousand million pounds. Included in the proposal was a 3.6 percent reduction in cereal prices. Andriessen based his proposal on three facts: Farm production in Europe was at a record high in 1984; farm income had grown at a high average of 4 percent in real terms, reversing its sharp fall in 1983; and most important, the EC was broke and would have to wait for several months to replenish its revenues until a 1985 budget was approved.

The British government supported Andriessen's price proposal. Jopling stated in the House of Commons that any significant increase in EC farm prices was irresponsible (*Times of London,* March 14, 1985:2). The chief source of opposition was Germany, represented by Kiechle, who adamantly refused to accept the 3.6 percent cut in cereal prices on the grounds that it would seriously reduce German farmers' incomes. He argued instead for a cereal price increase. German opposition caused the postponement of the April deadline for annual price fixing. Deliberations were suspended until after the crucial German elections in North Rhine–Westphalia scheduled for May 12.

Andriessen reacted angrily, calling Kiechle's attitude "unacceptable and contradictory." He claimed that Kiechle's proposals would cost the EC money that Kiechle's own colleague, the German finance minister, Gerhardt Stoltenberg, would oppose allocating. Speculation was that in order for Andriessen to gain support for his farm price proposals, Kiechle would have to be outvoted in the Council of Ministers. Such a development was certain, however, to be a prelude to Kiechle's ouster from the German cabinet. Furthermore, since the British were outvoted on an issue they regarded as being of national importance in 1982, Thatcher was expected to support Germany's right of veto on the grounds of principle.[4]

The outcome of the North Rhine–Westphalia elections reinforced Kiechle's refusal to budge on the proposed price cut on cereals. The coalition Social Democratic party government of Chancellor Helmut Kohl sustained a stinging defeat in the state elections and reacted by strongly supporting his agriculture minister on the price-cut issue. Kohl sent an angry message to Jacques Delors, the president of the EC Commission. In it he gave his full support to Kiechle's threat to veto any attempt to cut cereal prices and stated, "You have to learn it is not possible to put one of the most important member states under such pressure" (*Times of London*, May 15, 1985:7).

Andriessen's ambitious reform proposals failed when the EC agriculture ministers agreed to accede to the German demand for no meaningful cuts in the price of cereals. The Germans took the position that the "cereals crisis" was not due to their intransigence but rather to the production of low-quality crops by countries such as Britain. The significance of this outcome was that it upheld a principle that was destroying the CAP: that prices for EC food surpluses that were neither needed nor wanted would be supported nonetheless. As a consequence it would be virtually impossible to hold farm spending to within the agreed budget of twelve thousand million pounds for 1985.

Nevertheless, Andriessen and the EC Commission continued to press for "radical reforms" on cereal production (*Times of London*, July 17, 1985:6). Negotiations were to start in earnest in September 1985, when the first EEP sale was announced.

[4]Under the principle of majority voting in the Council of Ministers, the big four countries (Great Britain, France, Germany, and Italy) have 10 votes each. In descending order of size, the smaller countries have 5 votes each (Netherlands, Belgium, and Greece), 3 votes (Denmark and Ireland), or 2 votes (Luxembourg). Thus 45 votes would constitute a qualified majority vote in the Council of Ministers.

Chapter Six

The Political Impact of the EEP on the European Community

In 1986, Frans Andriessen proposed another freeze on the next season's agricultural prices, hoping to discourage surplus food production in the community.[1] He warned that agricultural surpluses were a time bomb that would destroy the Common Agricultural Policy, and he stressed that the community's £6,000 million food surplus had to be sold without disrupting agricultural markets. The cost of exporting that surplus could force the EC Commission to demand an additional £450 million for the 1986 budget, and even this estimate was optimistic, based, as it was, on the assumption that agricultural prices for the year would be frozen.

The prospects for Andriessen's proposal that year changed with the government in France. Jacques Chirac became the new prime minister and France entered an uneasy period of so-called cohabitation between the Socialist president Mitterrand and the Gaullist prime minister. Chirac had been a staunch supporter of French farmers since he was agriculture minister in 1972 under

---

[1] Andriessen did acknowledge, however, that under Article 39 of the Treaty of Rome, the EC is obliged to take into account the standard of living of the agricultural population when formulating agricultural policy and that farmers' incomes had not increased with those of the rest of the economy, a circumstance that posed a serious threat to the future of the small- and medium-sized family farms the CAP was concerned to protect (*Agra Europe*, February 7, 1986:P/5).

the Gaullist presidency of Georges Pompidou. Whatever French support for reforming the EC's farm policy there had been under the Socialist government of Mitterrand gave way to Chirac's commitment to support French farmers' demands. Mitterrand and the Socialists made no attempt to control Chirac's agricultural policies, recognizing that there were no votes to be won by alienating the farming industry. Any attempt to undercut Chirac in Brussels could only lose the Socialists votes in the rural areas without gaining them anything in the urban areas.

Chirac demonstrated his independence with his appointment of François Guillaume, the outspoken head of the French farmers' union, to the position of agriculture minister in his cabinet. The appointment created the improbable situation whereby the French agriculture minister would be meeting with EC farm ministers against whom he had previously led farmers' demonstrations in Brussels. Needless to say, fears rose among EC governments that they would soon be at odds with the French government over farm spending (*Times of London*, November 24, 1986:5).

The Path to Catastrophe

Guillaume lived up to his hard-line reputation. Just before his first meeting with the Council of Ministers in March 1986, he vowed to obtain a 4.7 percent farm price increase. He categorically rejected the Commission's farm price freeze, which had the backing of the United Kingdom, and he also declared that the Chirac government would never have agreed to the British budget concession negotiated at the Fontainebleau summit of 1984 (*Times of London*, March 27, 1986:7). Margaret Thatcher countered. During Britain's presidency of the EC (scheduled to begin in June 1986), the United Kingdom's priority, she declared, would be reform of the costly CAP. Guillaume, who had once called for Britain's withdrawal from the EC, retorted that as far as he was concerned, the principal objective of the CAP was to guarantee a higher income for European farmers (*Times of London*, March 27, 1986:7).

During the April meeting of the Council of Ministers, the

French and German governments sought to form a political alliance to block the commission's efforts to implement a price freeze for the 1986–87 marketing year. Guillaume tried to show some flexibility by arguing for a price rise of 1 percent instead of the 4.7 percent he had originally demanded, but the Germans resisted, opposing any price cuts. Both governments justified their opposition on the grounds that the commission's proposal would adversely affect their farmers (*Times of London*, April 23, 1986:9).

German agriculture minister Kiechle, speaking at the opening of International Green Week in Berlin in January 1986, said that he was committed to his policy of "increasing prices to cut production." In an interview with *Die Welt*, he asserted that farm income had been stagnant for ten years and that "brutal price pressure to throw the weaker farmer out of the market" was not the solution to the problem of surplus production. EC farm prices would have to retain their function of guaranteeing farmers' incomes, he said. The German government could not tell the average German farmer year after year that production must remain constant and that farm prices would not increase. Despite the fact that the German government paid DM 30 billion annually for its agricultural system, the income gap between the rural and urban areas was wider than ever, and to the detriment of farmers (*German Tribune*, February 16, 1986:6). Kiechle acknowledged therefore that if, because of the EC's tight budgetary situation, farm prices did not increase, then the German government would have to consider national measures to increase farmers' income (*Agra Europe*, January 24, 1986:P/4).

Kiechle's remarks were undoubtedly motivated by his perception of electoral threats to the ruling Christian Democratic Union and its Bavarian affiliate, the Christian Social Union. Christian Democratic Union politicians in Bonn were concerned that many farmers in the states of Saarland, North Rhine–Westphalia, Schleswig-Holstein, and Lower Saxony who were traditional supporters of the party would abstain or even cross over and vote for the opposition Social Democratic party or the Green party in impending elections.

French objectives in EC farm policy negotiations were complicated. On the one hand, Guillaume sought an all-round 4.7

percent price increase as demanded by COPA and the French farm syndicates. On the other hand, he sought, above all else, the dismantling of the green ECU system, since it was a major barrier to the full exploitation of France's comparative advantage as the principal agricultural producer in the European Community. This placed France in the ambivalent position of being willing to trade off farm price increases for even a partial dismantlement of Germany's green currency (that is, its positive MCAs).

Since any lowering of German MCAs would inevitably mean a lowering of German farmers' incomes, the German government's policy on that issue is inflexible.[2] These competing interests made for a very tenuous political alliance between France and Germany on EC farm policy. Speaking in 1986, Guillaume summarized the differences between the French and German governments on the CAP. He said that although both the French and the Germans wanted to raise farm prices, the German government was prepared to accept production quotas whereas the French were not. In addition, the German government was against the EC export policy whereas France strongly supported it. Guillaume went on to say that the French must "play our card for specialization" and that French cereal producers are the "best producers in the world" (*Le Monde*, May 27, 1986:25).

The French were also more confrontational than the Germans in dealing with U.S. demands that the EC negotiate the elimination of "protectionist" agricultural policies. For example, when the Reagan administration threatened trade retaliation if the community imposed restrictions on U.S. imports to Spain and Portugal once they joined the EC, claiming U.S. farmers would lose between seven hundred million and two billion dollars a year, the French external trade minister, Michel Noir, said that the Europeans' answer to Washington should be "an eye for an eye, a tooth for a tooth" (*German Tribune*, June 8, 1986:7).

The combined French and German opposition proved unable

[2]Under the terms of the 1984 Fontainebleau agreement, German and Dutch positive MCAs (designed to protect their national farmers from competition within the EC) were to be gradually eliminated over the three years from 1985 to 1988. The German government blocked all efforts to eliminate the green currency system, however.

to deter the Council of Ministers from finally agreeing on a farm price package that froze 1986–87 EC price guarantees to its farmers.[3] As it turned out, however, the farmers of all EC countries but Germany received a modest price rise as a result of the manipulation of the community's financial mechanism. Hidden price rises were achieved through the realignment of European currencies.

Since the German deutsche mark is the most important unit of currency in the EC, the ECU is in effect pegged to it. The ECU is based on a basket of European currencies in which, for example, in January 1987 the deutsche mark constituted 34.9 percent; the French franc, 19 percent; the Dutch guilder, 11 percent; and the Italian lire, 9.4 percent of the total value of the currency.

In April of 1986 the German government revalued (that is, increased the value of) the deutsche mark by 3 percent. Most other EC countries simultaneously devalued (that is, lowered the value of) their currencies against the mark. The effect of this action was to pass on to farmers in national currencies the higher ECU prices, except, of course, there was no differential to pass along to German farmers. It was not surprising, therefore, that Kiechle voted against (but did not veto) the EC's price freeze of April 26. Kiechle's tactic apparently was to ask the German government to "top up" the "frozen" EC farm prices to increase the income of German farmers. With state elections scheduled for late 1986 and with all-German elections in January 1987, Kiechle calculated that the government in Bonn would support his proposal to add to the EC subsidies (*Economist*, May 3, 1986:56).

Although the EC believed its 1986–87 farm price package would not increase pressure on its budget, it did face trouble from the fall of the U.S. dollar. In the 1986 draft budget, the ECU had been valued at $1.12, but by February 1986 the U.S. dollar

[3]The European farming organizations, COPA and COGECA, continued to oppose the commission's price freeze proposal as "totally unacceptable" given the dramatic fall in farmers' incomes, which fully justified an average price increase of 4.7 percent. They argued that acceptance of the proposals would inevitably increase the risk of renationalizing the CAP (*Agra Europe*, February 7, 1986: P/6).

had fallen to $1.02. The EC Commission had estimated it would have to request an additional 790 million ECUs from the Council of Ministers to meet export costs rising with the falling dollar and, moreover, might be forced to make another request in 1987 for supplementary funding to meet added budgetary requirements arising from the implementation of the 1985 U.S. farm bill (Agra Europe, February 7, 1986:P/1). By late March, however, the EC's budgetary situation had already worsened. Budget Commissioner Henning Christophersen had admitted that an additional 1.5 billion ECUs would be required to finance the costs of the CAP (Agra Europe, March 21, 1986:P/3).

Under the terms of the 1984 Fontainebleau agreement, the level of increase in EC expenditure could not go beyond approximately 6 percent. Under the 1986 agreement, that ceiling would be adhered to, but the community would require a supplementary budget for agriculture of about 2.5 billion ECUs, subject to approval by the EC finance ministers. Such a request can only be approved under "exceptional circumstances," and the grounds on which the additional funding was to be requested was the fall in the value of the U.S. dollar.

Export refunds, which had cost the EC about $5.1 billion in 1985, were expected to rise to $8.5 billion in 1986 for three reasons: a 30 percent drop in the value of the U.S. dollar, low world prices for agricultural commodities owing to surplus production and stagnant demand, and the U.S. Export Enhancement Program (Agra Europe, July 24, 1987:E/3). Willy de Clercq, the European commissioner for external relations, warned that the Europeans could not afford to last out a trade war with the United States (German Tribune, April 13, 1986:1); for with the U.S. dollar at a low level, American export subsidies cost less than European ones. Since the dollar began its decline in 1985, the European Community had been forced to plough about DM 4 billion more than intended into subsidizing European products down to world market price levels.

During the May 1987 meeting of the EC Agriculture Council, Andriessen warned that a "catastrophic situation" existed for the EAGGF guarantee fund. The total EAGGF guarantee deficit in 1987 would be about 4.4 billion ECUs, including a carry-over deficit of 700 million ECUs from 1986. Andriessen accused member states of "budgetary schizophrenia" in that they were blind to the insolvent situation the EC was currently in and were only concerned with finding ways of spending more money rather than saving it (*Agra Europe*, May 29, 1987:P/2). If the Council of Ministers was to maintain financing for the EC through 1987, it would have to approve a supplementary budget to cover the roughly 5 billion ECU deficit. Since, however, there were only about 650 million ECUs legally available in the EC's "own resources" beyond the original 1987 budget, the ministers would have to find most of the money elsewhere.

Three measures were proposed. The first and most obvious was to use the 650 million ECUs still available to the EC from the 1.4 percent value-added tax (VAT) revenue base. The second was to switch EAGGF payments to member states from advances to arrears ("a posteriori reimbursement"); so that EAGGF expenditures for November and December of 1987 would be transferred to the 1988 budget account. The third measure was for the EC finance ministers to authorize an additional budget contribution above the 1.4 percent VAT limit. There was general support for the first two measures but considerable opposition, especially from the British government, to the third. It was clear, furthermore, that short of major CAP reform, including a price freeze and reduction in export subsidies, only the third measure could provide any hope of a long-term solution to the EC's budget crisis.

At the June 1987 summit meeting at Brussels, Thatcher vetoed the commission's efforts, known as the Delors plan (after the president of the EC Commission, Jacques Delors) to expand the revenue base from the VAT to a percentage of member countries' gross national product. The plan proposed that EC contributions be based on member countries' "relative prosperity" and "economic performance." Germany was by far the community's biggest net contributor, but Britain also paid more into the community budget than it received through the EC's various funds. Other member countries, however, including Denmark and the three Benelux countries with high per capita income levels, were net beneficiaries. The Delors plan would have obliged the latter countries to pay more to the community.

Budget Crisis

With CAP expenditures reaching an all-time high and with the EC's "own resources" exhausted, the February 1988 Brussels summit meeting of heads of state resulted in a virtual deadlock on the issue of spending controls on agriculture. The conflict was between the British government, on the one hand, and the French and German governments on the other. Britain took the position that the future level of EC farm spending should be pegged at nineteen thousand million pounds a year (excluding the costs of disposing of food surplus). Thatcher said that food surplus was the EC's chief problem and one the community had failed to face up to since 1980. The French and Germans sought to deflect the British argument while calling once more for increased agricultural spending.

The major sticking point in the budget controversy, however, was over maximum guaranteed levels of cereals production. Thatcher argued that the maximum guaranteed quantity (MGQ) for cereals production must be 155 million metric tons. EC heads of government had, she insisted, an obligation to taxpayers to limit surplus cereal production, because by her calculations, every 1 million metric tons over and above the ceiling would cost the EC an additional 400 million pounds a year between 1988 and 1992 (*Times of London*, February 13, 1988:6). The French and German governments insisted on a limit of 160 million metric tons on the grounds that it was necessary to guarantee the incomes of their small farmers. Chirac said he would not settle for less. Coincidentally, both France and Germany faced impending elections and thus were under pressure to demonstrate to their agricultural voters that they were championing farmers' interests in EC negotiations.

The political significance of this controversy was largely symbolic, however. A difference of 5 million metric tons in the MGQ for cereals would not in itself significantly reduce expenditures. For example, a cereal harvest of 168 million metric tons (production has exceeded 160 only twice in EC history) with a 155 million metric ton MGQ would only produce a maximum saving of 233 million ECUs out of a CAP budget of over 28 billion ECUs (*Agra Europe*, February 5, 1988:P/4). The real significance of imposing limits on cereal production was that it would be the first attempt to apply strict, automatic controls to surplus production. The cereal controversy took on added significance because the cereals sector was expected to be the most costly item in the 1989 CAP budget. A projected EAGGF expenditure for cereals of 5.428 billion ECUs would top the perennially most costly dairy products expenditure, projected to be 4.85 billion ECUs in 1989 (*Agra Europe*, July 29, 1988:E/2).

The deadlock turned acrimonious. Chirac criticized Thatcher for acting like a "housewife" when she demanded that the EC follow strict budgetary discipline and that EC members give iron-clad guarantees of reductions in farm spending. He then used the word *couilles* (bollocks) to describe her after she accused him of obstructing the summit. Thatcher responded that Chirac's behavior had been "unbelievable" and that only a Frenchman could have acted in such a manner (*Times of London*, February 15, 1988:7).

Compromise

A compromise agreement was finally reached in mid-February. As in any compromise, the major parties to the conflict gained enough to be able to present political achievements to their national constituencies. On the crucial issue of legally binding limits to agricultural spending, Thatcher claimed a victory. The Brussels agreement set a spending limit of £19.25 thousand million for 1988, just in excess of the £19 thousand million limit Britain had called for. This limit was authorized to rise to £20.72 thousand million by 1991. On the issue of ceilings on the MGQ for cereals, however, Thatcher was forced to give ground. The agreement called for a cereals MGQ of 160 million metric tons per year for the next four years instead of the 155 million the British had originally insisted on. Even so, it was something of a victory for the British in that automatic cuts were accepted for the first time. Known as a "budgetary stabilizer," the mechanism sets ceilings on the quantity of a particular commodity that the EC will fully subsidize.[4] For cereals, an automatic cumulative price cut of 3 percent was to go into effect as soon as the 160 million metric ton limit should be exceeded.

To finance the increased cost of the EC budget, the Brussels summit authorized a new method of financing the community— the Delors plan—whereby the twelve members would be assessed on the basis of gross national product. By 1992, member states were to be contributing 1.2 percent of the EC's gross national product, the equivalent of a VAT of about 1.9 percent, as compared to the 1987 VAT of 1.4 percent. The new system would reduce the inequitable bias against the British and thereby eliminate, supposedly, a nagging source of political tension. It seemed possible, however, that once the British net contribution had declined significantly, other members might begin to press the United Kingdom to give up its hard-won budget compensation granted at Fontainebleau in 1984.

Within the compromise agreement on the Delors plan lay the seeds of more political dissension; for although the new so-called fourth resource of the community (the percentage of GNP) would work to the advantage of the new member states—Spain and Portugal—it had the potential to penalize others seriously. The accession of Spain and Portugal to the EC had shifted the political power within the community. Before 1986, the "rich" member states in the north always dominated. Then in 1986, the Italian premier, Bettino Craxi, had made it clear that the community's southern members expected the "northerners" to finance the 1987 budget deficit because they received the lion's share of the benefits (*German Tribune*, December 14, 1986:1). By 1988, the southerners (to whom the Irish could be added from time

---

[4]Comparable budgetary stabilizers were also agreed to for oilseeds and protein plants: rapeseed, sunflower seeds, soya beans, and peas, beans, and lupins grown for animal feed. Production ceilings on all these commodities were set higher than originally requested by the British.

to time) had a blocking minority that could make life difficult for the Germans, French, Dutch, and Danes. The north, led by France and Germany, wanted to retain a structure by which agricultural expenditure accounted for roughly two-thirds of budget spending. The south, along with Ireland, insisted on much higher structural fund expenditure.

The EC Commission outlined a medium-term proposal for the period until 1993, when the Single European Act for a uniform internal market was slated to be implemented. The commission recommended increasing EC contributions by 25 percent, limiting CAP expenditure to 50 percent of the budget, and doubling the structural fund's allocations. The idea behind the proposal was to reduce the gap between the rich industrial north and the poor agricultural south in order for the EC to become a genuine European Community. However enlightened and farsighted the proposal, declining agricultural budget resources and increasing demands remained a threat.

Reduced Pressure on the EC Budget

Before the political solution formulated at the 1988 Brussels summit could be tested, an unexpected event outside of the European Community's control intervened to remove, at least temporarily, the growing pressure on the EC budget: the prolonged and extreme drought in the United States, which severely damaged wheat and coarse-grain crops in the summer of 1988. By mid-July the drought was expected to reduce U.S. wheat yields by at least 30 percent. This estimate, together with the fact of depletion of stocks of wheat and coarse grains during the 1987–88 season, pushed the international price of wheat up by more than 20 percent. According to the International Wheat Council, the world wheat price rose to over $145 per metric ton at the end of June 1988 (compared with a base level of $100 per metric ton from July to December 1986). The world stocks of wheat and coarse grains were expected to fall during the 1988–89 marketing year, and indeed, U.S. production of wheat declined from 57.4 million metric tons in 1987–88 to 49.3 million in 1988–89 (HGCA *Weekly Digest*, May 22, 1989:1). Hence the

Figure 6.1. 1988 EC wheat export refunds. From *Agra Europe*, July 29, 1988: P/1.

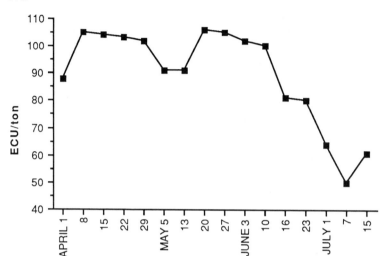

world prices of wheat and coarse grain were expected to remain relatively high at least until the 1989 Northern Hemisphere harvest.

So sudden adverse weather conditions in the United States gave the EC a temporary respite from the budgetary consequences of failing to deal with its chronic surpluses in the cereals sector. Along with savings in the dairy sector, the reduction in wheat export refunds would enable the EC for the first time since 1984 to stay within its EAGGF budget spending limit. For example, the total EAGGF spending in the 1989 budget year was 28.1 billion ECUs, well within the 1989 budget authorization of 28.6 billion ECUs. The high world wheat prices significantly contributed to this outcome. Figure 6.1 shows a significant reduction in EC wheat export refunds from April to July 1988—a reduction of about 50 percent, from 89 ECUs per metric ton in April to approximately 48 ECUs per metric ton in July. This decline in EC export refunds corresponded to an equally significant decline in U.S. export subsidies for grain during the same period (see Figures 4.1 and 4.2).

Although the 1988 U.S. drought gave the EC a breathing spell from the political pressure of chronic budget crisis, there was reason to believe that relief would be only temporary, because the EC did not bring its surplus cereal production problem under control. The 1988 production of grain was 164 million metric tons, or 4 million more than the limit; yet the high world prices and the loopholes in the penalties for over production (exemptions for smaller producers) resulted in no overproduction penalty that year. The EC actually took advantage of the situation to expand grain exports substantially. The community licensed about 600 million bushels of soft wheat for export in 1988, almost double the 1987 amount. EC barley export licenses increased by 30 percent, corn licenses by 130 percent (*Agweek*, May 22, 1989:25). High prices and a shortage of U.S. wheat further stimulated overproduction and the accumulation of more exportable surpluses.

Drought's end in the United States during 1990 brought bumper grain crops. With increasing cereal production almost everywhere, grain prices could only fall again, leading to renewed dissension in the EC and renewed U.S. interest in the EEP as a retaliatory trade policy.

Chapter Seven

The EEP as a Bargaining Lever
in the GATT Negotiations

During the Reagan administration, the United States and the European Community followed two diametrically opposed agricultural philosophies. The Europeans took the position that governments must provide a floor for agricultural prices in order to maintain a minimum income for farmers. The United States believed that agricultural production should be geared to marketplace forces and farmers should be subject to the principle of the "survival of the fittest." Underlying this philosophical conflict was the fact that the farm population and its political lobby were vastly more powerful in Europe than in the United States. In 1989 the U.S. farm population was estimated to be only 2 million, whereas there were more than 11 million farmers in Europe.

The Reagan administration was determined to persuade Europe to modify its agricultural policy, and the Export Enhancement Program was its preferred diplomatic bargaining tool because of its inherent advantage over other programs.[1] Unlike the

[1]The set-aside program is designed to limit agricultural production by restricting the use of farmland, specifically, the area of a farmer's total cropland base used for production. Closely related to the set-aside program is the acreage reduction program, under which the secretary of agriculture proclaims acreage reduction goals for specific crops. The size of the reduction is based on the

[1 1 5]

set-aside program, for example, which could only be implemented during the next planting season and with unpredictable results, the Export Enhancement Program had a direct and immediate impact on the European Community's highly controversial CAP budget. The Reagan administration threatened to support the inclusion of highly protectionist measures in the 1990 U.S. farm bill should the EC not agree to substantial reductions in its export subsidies. The reason the EEP had such a prominent role in the American strategy was that the EC had control not only over cereals but over other important agricultural markets such as dairy and meats. Yet it was through the cereals market that any lowering of prices would place the CAP budget under serious pressure. And since the EC did not have a financial margin to adjust to major changes, any substantial lowering of world grain prices (i.e., U.S. prices) would create a major financial problem for the European Community. A measure of the EEP's effectiveness was that in response to the threat of expanding the program to include other agricultural commodities in the 1990 U.S. farm bill, the European Community reluctantly agreed to place its agricultural export subsidy program on the GATT agenda for the first time—quite a reversal after years of implacable opposition to any discussion of export subsidies in the context of the GATT.

Critics question whether the EEP brought about the change. French government officials argue, for example, that the EEP contributed only about 300 million ECUs to the cost of the 1988 community budget, which at the time had a deficit of 5 billion ECUs (private communication from Jean-Baptiste Danel, agricultural counselor to the embassy of France in the United States, December 10, 1990). The program, they assert, only made things "a little more difficult." It is too easy, however, to minimize the impact of the EEP when the EC has just enjoyed a respite from budget pressure thanks to the North American drought, which put the EC in the fortunate and unexpected position in 1988–89 of having a financial surplus of as much as 4 billion ECUs with

amount of a crop (taking account of carry-over stocks from previous years and imports) that will be required to supply a given year's consumption, export, and reserve requirements.

which to offset its deficit. One can only speculate about the political fallout in the EC had there been no drought and had community governments been forced to deal with a 5 billion ECU deficit. The EEP's contribution to budget pressures would then have been much more noticeable.

U.S. government officials take a different view of the EEP's impact on the European Community. They concede that it cannot be shown empirically that the EEP caused the EC to negotiate more seriously in the Uruguay round, but they believe there is no doubt that the EEP, along with other U.S. actions such as lower loan rates and market access to government-owned and -controlled grain stocks, did put budget pressure on the EC in the latter part of the 1980s. The program did impose additional budget and transaction costs on the EC and showed that they could no longer do business as usual (private communication from James Vertrees, USDA Economic Research Service, December 17, 1990). Furthermore, if the United States had continued under the 1985 farm bill its policy of high loan rates, large government stocks, and acreage reduction programs without the EEP, it would have made it easier and far less costly for the EC and other exporting countries to increase production and exports at the expense of the United States. The failure of the Uruguay round of the GATT to achieve significant agricultural reform therefore disposes the U.S. government toward greater use of the EEP and other programs to expand U.S. exports and to keep the budgetary pressures on the European Community.

The Struggle over the GATT Agenda

A well-known irony of the U.S. effort to persuade the EC and Japan to discontinue their "trade-distorting" practices in agriculture is that the United States itself was largely responsible for exempting agriculture from GATT's jurisdiction. The principal U.S. farm legislation is the Agricultural Adjustment Act of 1933, into which an additional provision, often referred to as Section 22, was incorporated in 1935. This provision empowered the president to impose import quotas on agricultural commodities to protect the U.S. farm industry from the adverse effects of farm imports. Section 22 import quotas are still used today to protect a wide range of U.S. farm commodities. The act was designed to restore and stabilize U.S. agriculture, which had been suffering from the effects of the Depression. It authorized state intervention to control agricultural production and to keep price supports above world levels. It also empowered the Commodity Credit Corporation to subsidize agricultural exports to increase or retain U.S. markets.

When the GATT agreement was concluded in 1947, the EC did not exist, the Japanese economy had not recovered from the devastation of World War II, and most Third World countries were still under colonial control. Given the dominance of the United States in the world economy, it is not surprising that the GATT rules governing trade in general, and agricultural trade in particular, were largely tailored to meet American domestic and foreign economic policy needs. In effect, the GATT agreement was designed to accommodate U.S. farm policy. While the GATT treaty was being drafted in 1947, U.S. negotiators were able to write in special rules for agriculture. Signatories to Article XI were allowed to impose agricultural import controls to protect their domestic farm industries. They were also allowed to restrict farm exports during times of severe shortages.

The United States also wrote special provisions into the GATT agreement to exempt agriculture from the general prohibition against export subsidies. The original GATT treaty did not proscribe export subsidies. Article XVI:4 was added later to prohibit export subsidies on all products *except* primary agricultural commodities. The only restriction on subsidizing agricultural exports is found in Article XVI:3, which states that a contracting state may not employ agricultural export subsidies to secure more than an "equitable share of world trade." Although numerous efforts have been made to define exactly what constitutes an equitable share of the world market and to determine when the principle of market-sharing equity has been violated, all such attempts have failed.[2]

---

[2]For a discussion of the U.S. role in ensuring that GATT rules were consistent with U.S. farm policy see Johnson (1950), Dam (1970), and Hillman (1978).

As the Reagan administration saw it, change was long over-due. It launched its major international initiative in September of 1986, to be pursued at the new round of GATT talks—the eighth, called the Uruguay round. In October 1986, seventy-eight countries met in Punta del Este, Uruguay, to begin the talks. They established a schedule for trade negotiations on ser-vices, agriculture, textiles, and tropical products, to take place over four years and conclude at the end of 1990. In December 1990, however, the round was extended one more year, until the end of 1991. The United States set three conditions for its par-ticipation: the EC should agree to negotiate the elimination of export subsidies; agricultural issues should be placed on a "fast track" for speedy negotiations; and negotiations should be based on the recommendations for liberalizing farm trade accepted by the GATT countries in 1984.

The first document the United States introduced was a pro-posal for GATT negotiations to eliminate all domestic national farm programs. The administration recommended complete elimination of all programs, including price supports, import controls, and supply management, within ten years. The EC's reaction was predictably hostile and negative. None of the GATT participants evinced any interest in dealing with anything so radical as the Reagan proposal. The EC external relations com-missioner, Willy de Clercq, referred to it as the "fast track" to agricultural trade reform and said the European Community would "not bow to pressure" to reach an early agreement (*Agra Europe*, March 27, 1987:P/4). He pointed out that the EC did not regard agriculture as any more urgent than trade reform in, for example, manufactured goods, and he insisted on sticking to the original four-year schedule for negotiating general trade reforms. The EC's position was that GATT talks on farm trade reform were inseparable from talks on other trade reform issues.

Frans Andriessen, the EC agriculture commissioner, claimed the U.S. proposal was "impractical" and went "too far too fast" (*Agra Europe*, July 24, 1987:P/1). The European Community, he said, rejected the premise underlying the proposal: that export subsidies could only be reduced if domestic agricultural pro-duction were also reduced proportionately. He stressed that the

[119]

EC would continue to fight for its right to dump surplus farm production on the world market.[3] Whatever agreement might be reached on reducing subsidies, the European Community would retain a dual pricing system.

While the EC was prepared to reduce its level of agricultural subsidies, it took the position that there was a gap between rhetoric and reality in the Reagan administration's attitude toward free trade in agriculture. In the European view, Washington was just as protectionist in farm trade as the European Community, and furthermore, American politicians would find Reagan's radical reform proposal just as difficult to carry out as European governments.

Although the United States had warned the EC that refusal to negotiate the CAP policy of subsidizing agricultural exports could jeopardize the entire trade talks, the EC was determined that the agenda for the GATT talks exclude any reference to the European Community's willingness to phase out export refunds. This position was largely attributable to strong French resistance. France regarded export refunds as untouchable (*Agra Europe*, July 25, 1986:P/3) and had made its position clear well before the Uruguay round began. At the Bonn Summit back in May 1985, French president Mitterrand had rejected Reagan's proposal for a new round of trade negotiations under GATT's auspices in 1986. Edith Cresson, then minister for foreign trade and industry, explained Mitterrand's decision in an address to the Trade Policy Research Center in London in June. She said the United States, the principal proponent of the new round, had not clearly outlined the agenda it would like to see addressed, whereas the European Community's Council of Ministers had openly called for a new GATT round based on what she referred to as the "real problems" confronting the international community: the erratic fluctuation in the value of the U.S. dollar and the large and continuing trade deficits with Japan (Cresson, 1985: 317–19).

Cresson doubted the Americans' reason for wanting early

[3]Dumping is defined as selling commodities on foreign markets at prices below those on the domestic market.

trade negotiations: to deflect internal pressure for protectionist legislation in Congress. Since the same pressure existed in the European Community, had for some time, and could be expected to continue, the "urgency" appeared suspect. Furthermore, the proposed GATT negotiations were expected to last between six and eight years. The Americans, she advised, should work out a convincing agenda before pressing to set a date for a new round. The minister also noted that William Brock, the U.S. trade representative, had testified before the joint Economic Committee in Congress that under the Reagan administration, more restrictive trade measures had been adopted than during the previous four administrations. His testimony raised a very real question of logical consistency: How could the United States press the GATT negotiations for liberalizing trade and at the same time adopt restrictive trade practices?

During the preliminary discussions in Geneva just before the Uruguay round, France had insisted on separating the EC's system of export refunds from any negotiations on farm trade. It had refused, for example, to accept the EC draft of a GATT ministerial declaration submitted by Switzerland and Colombia which included among other things the provision that a separate group be established to address GATT "subsidies and countervailing duties." The French feared that the creation of a group to negotiate subsidies and countervailing duties would raise the subject of farm export subsidies and thereby link farm trade and export refunds in the GATT negotiations. The French government stood by its refusal to allow export subsidies to be on the GATT agenda.

Clayton Yeutter, the U.S. trade representative at the time, was highly critical of the French position. He maintained that neither France nor the EC had anything to fear in the proposed draft declaration. He went on to say, however, that in response to "pushy EC trade policies" (implying export subsidies), the United States had decided to take a more confrontational attitude (*Agra Europe*, September 5, 1986:P/3). In fact, Yeutter subsequently explained the political role of the EEP in relation to the GATT talks in just such terms. During his confirmation hearings before the Senate Agriculture Committee in 1989, he

[121]

said that the Export Enhancement Program was effective in enabling the United States to reclaim wheat markets lost to the EC, though he conceded that the program, like the European Community's export subsidies, did "distort trade enormously." He believed, nonetheless, that the United States needed export subsidies in order to neutralize the EC as long as it subsidized EC exports (*Agweek*, February 13, 1989:42). Yeutter even threatened to walk out of the Uruguay round if the EC did not agree to negotiate the elimination of export subsidies in the GATT talks.

Despite pressure from Yeutter, however, de Clercq, refused to budge, arguing that the GATT trade talks should not focus on a single issue. He said that on no account could the "fundamental mechanism" of CAP be called into question in negotiations (*Agra Europe*, September 12, 1986:P/6), and he countered with the assertion that the EC wanted to discuss other types of farm subsidies, including the U.S. deficiency payments to farmers and the Canadian government's transport subsidies for grain farmers.

The United States was not alone in attempting to pressure the EC to negotiate the elimination of export subsidies in the Uruguay round. Pressure came as well from the Cairns Group of so-called fair trade countries. Higgott and Cooper (1990) have described the group as a coalition of small "nonsubsidizing" agriculture-exporting nations of the world that were hit hard by the U.S.-EC grain subsidy war. The group sought to play the role of go-between and consensus builder in the Uruguay round. Its members were Argentina, Australia, Brazil, Canada, Colombia, Chile, Fiji, Hungary, Indonesia, Malaysia, New Zealand, the Philippines, Thailand, and Uruguay. The most vocal of them was Australia, which was labeled (along with the United States) as one of the two hawks of the GATT farm trade lobby.

Although the fair traders criticized both the United States and the European Community for engaging in a farm export subsidy war, they primarily blamed the EC for starting the war, and they supported the American demand that the European Community include export subsidies on the GATT agenda (Higgott and Cooper, 1990:623). The Australian prime minister, Bob Hawke, averred that the large subsidies the EC funded each year to market its agricultural exports forced the Reagan administration to retaliate by subsidizing its own exports under the Export Enhancement Program (*Agra Europe*, August 29, 1986:P/1). Roberts places a somewhat different interpretation on Hawke's statement: that the prime minister did not mean to justify the EEP but meant only that the U.S. retaliation was "understandable" in the light of the EC export subsidies (private communication, October 17, 1990). Nevertheless, the result is the same. The Australians as well as the rest of the Cairns Group and others have blamed the EC for the grain subsidy war, as they also blamed the community for the breakdown of the Uruguay round in 1991.

The Australians organized the fourteen-country trade alliance in August of 1986 in order to exert diplomatic pressure for an end to the U.S.-EC agricultural trade war; for they were concerned that they would become its victims. The Australian government claimed that Australia had lost about one billion dollars annually for several years because of the CAP (Australian Bureau of Agricultural and Resource Economics, 1986), and the Australian federal minister for primary industry, John Kerin, said that U.S.-EC agricultural subsidies would cost Australian farmers 33 percent of their net income during 1987 and 43 percent during 1988 (*Agra Europe*, July 4, 1986:P/3).

The Cairns Group issued the "Cairns Declaration" at the conclusion of a meeting in Cairns, Australia, just before the September 1986 Uruguay round was scheduled to meet in Punta del Este. The declaration called for the removal of barriers to the access to agricultural markets; for substantial reductions in agricultural subsidies; and for the ultimate elimination of all agricultural subsidies affecting trade, to be achieved within an agreed period. In effect, the Cairns Group supported the U.S. demand for completely eliminating trade-distorting subsidies within ten years. Yet rather than risk terminating GATT negotiations over an impasse, they thought it better to take a medium-term, pragmatic position and negotiate reductions in trade subsidies that could later lead to total elimination. The fair traders therefore proposed that the United States and the EC accept an immediate freeze on trade subsidies and then negotiate a 10 percent annual reduction.

Just before the resumption of the Uruguay round in Geneva in

[123]

September 1987, the agricultural ministers from the Americas, including Canada, Latin America, and the Caribbean states, also declared their support for the U.S. position. Although the thirty-nine countries represented at the Inter-American Conference stopped short of endorsing the U.S. demand that all subsidies end by the year 2000, they did endorse the U.S. goal of ending subsidies (*Agra Europe*, September 4, 1987:P/1).

Maneuvering in the Uruguay Round

The reason all efforts to negotiate agricultural trade before Punta del Este had failed was that neither the EC nor the United States was prepared to discuss the basic principles of its trade policy. The EC had refused to discuss its CAP policy, and the United States had refused to discuss its "waiver" policy whereby it operated any frontier policy it chose. Thus it was a major breakthrough when, just before the round formally opened, trade ministers from ninety-two countries finally agreed to a joint declaration to discuss the core issue of export subsidies. This final declaration largely reflected the demands of the Cairns Group, in that though it did not single out the EC's export subsidies for negotiation, it did include a commitment to phase out all export subsidies. Pointing out the significance of this statement, the Australian minister of trade, John Dawkins, said that the EC's export refunds would be on the GATT agenda (*Agra Europe*, September 26, 1986:P/4). The declaration also implied the inclusion of U.S. subsidies, but it was clearly targeted at negotiating reductions in the CAP.

There was little optimism at first that real progress could be expected, given the European Community's seeming failure to understand the almost universal resentment toward the effects of the CAP—a point driven home by the EC's initial negotiating position that agricultural surpluses were a worldwide phenomena that should be negotiated. The EC therefore proposed that a cartel of major exporting countries manage the production of agricultural commodities on the basis of a market-sharing formula and made this proposal a precondition for negotiating reductions in export subsidies. Frans Andriessen said, for example, that the EC would like to end the "subsidy race," but this meant a certain amount of market sharing. The Americans rejected the concept of market sharing as a device for carving up world farm trade on the grounds that not only did it not work but it also failed to address the underlying problem of surplus production (*Agra Europe*, November 7, 1986:P/2). The United States held to its doctrinaire liberal trade theory rejection of a mercantilist approach and its insistence that all "trade-distorting" subsidies end by the year 2000.

Speaking for the Reagan administration, Under Secretary Daniel Amstutz said that the United States had no interest in any market-sharing arrangements to "carve up world agricultural trade" (*Agra Europe*, November 7, 1986:P/2). He pointed out that the United States had already tried this unsuccessfully in relation to the International Dairy Arrangement and saw no advantages to such a venture. Attempts to correct the distortions in domestic agricultural policies before attacking the international problems had failed to work in the past, he said, so the Reagan administration proposed to first eliminate trade distortions in GATT negotiations and then bring domestic agricultural policy into line with the international agreements. The United States backed a freeze on agricultural subsidies followed by a complete phase-out. These two diametrically opposed positions left no room for compromise.

Pressure Works

The United States adopted a strategy of negotiation by ultimatum; that is to say, it used the threat of strong action in response to a breakdown in negotiations. Not only did Clayton Yeutter threaten to walk out of the GATT session, but he also said that the EC's failure to negotiate an elimination of subsidies would trigger legislative action in the U.S. Congress on some extremely protectionist measures. The EC proposal to include all "direct and indirect subsidies" in the discussions within "an agreed time frame" pointedly omitted any mention of the phased removal of subsidies. Yeutter called the proposal unacceptable because it did not meet the U.S. demand for the elimination of subsidies to be negotiated by the end of 1990; the Cairns Group rejected it because it did not provide for substantial reductions in subsidies leading to total elimination by an agreed time.

When the EC rejected the U.S. proposal to eliminate agricultural protection by the year 2000, which Andriessen called politically unworkable, the U.S. Senate, by a vote of 71–27, approved a trade bill containing tough retaliatory measures designed to increase pressure on the EC in the GATT round. The bill authorized massive export subsidies for U.S. grain and oilseeds beginning in 1990. There was also growing sentiment in Congress for the expansion of the EEP to include maize in retaliation for EC subsidies for maize exports. Because the Reagan administration had called for a freeze and elimination of all subsidies, the Congress did not, however, grant these vastly expanded subsidies outright; instead it gave the EC an opportunity to negotiate reductions within GATT and gave the president the power to wave the implementation of the subsidies by certifying that progress was being made. In response to criticism from the Cairns Group that the EEP was damaging their economies, Tom Kay, the USDA Foreign Agricultural Service administrator, asserted that the Export Enhancement Program had brought the EC to the bargaining table, so the United States would not declare a "cease fire" until the European Community had done so. Washington had to keep up the pressure to the "greatest degree possible" (Agra Europe, August 7, 1987:P/5).

The fall in the value of the U.S. dollar and the growing CAP budget forced the EC to make a major diplomatic concession to the Reagan administration. By late 1987, the total CAP spending was expected to be roughly 30 billion ECUs, 18 billion of which would be for export refunds. Because export subsidies were denominated in U.S. dollars, any fall in the value of the dollar meant increased payments. If domestic prices were maintained, the gap between the domestic prices and the lower world price would have to be made up with export refunds. An 11 percent fall in the value of the U.S. dollar would therefore increase the cost of subsidizing EC exports by almost 2 billion ECUs in 1987.

For example, whereas in 1984 when the value of the U.S. dollar was high in relation to the deutsche mark–dominated ECU, the EC could export its grain at a near-zero refund rate, maximum refunds for wheat had risen by October of 1987 to approximately $150 per metric ton (*Agra Europe*, December 11, 1987:P/5). In addition to this dramatic rise in the cost of export subsidies, the September 1987 stock market crash made the European Community concerned over the spiraling costs of subsidizing exports. The fear was that the crash would have a global impact, depress demand, and thus further lower the price of agricultural commodities, thereby adding to the burden of financing the CAP budget and the consequent political difficulties.

In October 1987, therefore, the EC submitted a negotiating position paper to the GATT agricultural committee in Geneva in order to bring "an end to the subsidy war." It contained two proposals: (1) an initial plan to "prevent disruption" of the international market through agreement on minimum prices and market sharing plus a scaling down of support, and (2) a longer term undertaking to reduce subsidies and a commitment in principle to separate income support from agricultural production. The United States was unhappy with the first proposal but cheered by the second.

The Americans strongly opposed the first proposal because in their opinion it was institutionalized mercantilism. In other words, it reflected the French export-driven policy of protecting politically vulnerable industries by obtaining concessions for exports. For example, the European Community demanded that it be allowed to exchange reductions in cereal export refunds and import levies for the right to impose restrictions on the imports of U.S. cereal substitutes (such as corn gluten and soya). The concept of market sharing implied managing the control of markets for agricultural export commodities through a cartel of major exporters. Although Andriessen had said, "We must put an end to the subsidy war," he meant to do so through market sharing that would grant the European Community between 14 and 16 percent of the world cereal market (*Agra Europe*, October 9, 1987:E/1), a significant reduction from its 22 percent share.

The EC remained determined to defend its markets from threats posed by climate, production cycles, world monetary policies, or competition from other exporters. Guy Legras, the European Community Commission's director general for agriculture, characterized the U.S. and Cairns Group proposals as neither workable nor practical because they left the 11 million EC farmers without protection from the disastrous consequences of market forces. "One cannot," he insisted, "brutally force things down farmers' throats, the lives of millions are at stake" (*Agra Europe*, October 30, 1987:P/2).

Washington was, however, encouraged by the EC's proposal to cut farm subsidies and its agreement in principle to separate farmers' income support from their agricultural production. In late October, Washington hailed the EC's endorsement of the U.S. demands, declaring it a "major departure" from the European Community's original position. U.S. agriculture secretary Richard Lyng said in London in early November that he found "some common ground" between the protagonists in Geneva. He even predicted an agreement in principle before the end of 1988 (*Agra Europe*, November 6, 1987:E/6). The opinion in Washington was that the aggressive U.S. trade strategy was producing positive results in the GATT negotiations. The tangible evidence was that the EC had made concessions to the United States on the Spanish feed grain import controversy and other items in a U.S./EC agreement (*Agra Europe*, December 4, 1987: P/6).[4] The expectation was that continued pressure in the form of U.S. export subsidies would eventually restore the United States to dominance over world agricultural markets.

Negotiations Stall

Within six months of this optimistic appraisal, however, the prospects for a farm trade agreement in the Uruguay round

[4] As a consequence of being admitted to the EC in 1986, Spain had to increase its tariff on grain from the United States. The latter reacted sharply to this attempt to deny it markets in Spain and threatened to retaliate by imposing a 200 percent import duty on selected European agricultural exports. The EC capitulated and withdrew the proposed tariff increase (*Economist*, January 31, 1987:14–15).

seemed remote. From the U.S. perspective, negotiations had stalled because the EC was no longer under financial pressure to negotiate an end to the subsidy war. In March 1988, Amstutz declared that the recent reduction in U.S. farm spending and the resolution of the EC budget crisis had weakened the pressure on the United States and the EC to negotiate a farm trade agreement (*Agra Europe*, March 18, 1988:P/3).

Then in April the U.S. drought began to work to the EC's benefit. First, it created an excellent opportunity for European exporters to regain cereal market shares lost to the United States because of the EEP. The speculation within the European Community was that if rains did not arrive soon, the United States would be forced to abandon deliveries to less strategic markets such as Mexico and Spain. The U.S. administration was greatly concerned that America might not be able to defend newly regained markets. Second, the EC Commission was able sharply to reduce its export refunds, thus alleviating pressure on the European budget.

The U.S. administration had always realized that the Export Enhancement Program by itself would not be sufficient to persuade the European Community to negotiate farm trade agreements. It was designed to work in combination with other factors such as the decline in the value of the U.S. dollar and rising political tension over financing the CAP budget. The drought in 1988 and 1989 tipped the balance in the GATT talks in favor of the EC. The increase in the prices of key agricultural commodities temporarily contained the spiraling costs of export subsidies, removing the incentive for the European Community to negotiate a trade reform agreement with the United States.

After four days of stalemate at the midterm of the Uruguay round in Montreal in December of 1988, the negotiations broke down. The deadlock occurred after the Cairns Group became angry over the lack of progress in U.S.-EC negotiations on agriculture and threatened to block any other agreement at the GATT talks until there was an agreement on agricultural subsidies. The United States reacted strongly. Senator Patrick Leahy, the chairman of the Senate Agriculture Committee, threatened to push for a strong "export-oriented farm bill" in 1990 unless there was progress in the agricultural negotiations of the Uruguay round (*Agweek*, December 12, 1988:21). He asserted that despite pressures in Congress to reduce the deficit, there would be room for export subsidies in the federal budget. Indeed, Congress removed the ceiling on funding the Export Enhancement Program and included the EEP in the 1990 U.S. farm bill.

Although the EEP was effective as a diplomatic bargaining tool only when U.S. grain supplies were large, world prices low, competition keen, the value of the U.S. dollar low, and most crucially, political tension over the burgeoning CAP budget high, nevertheless, a U.S. recovery from the drought and renewed political tensions in the EC will undoubtedly make the Export Enhancement Program an effective lever in future GATT negotiations. What is essential is to recognize the limiting conditions under which a mercantilist economic policy is an effective political instrument. Failure to do so could be counterproductive; for it might well provoke retaliation without winning any strategic political advantage.

Conclusion

A mercantilist policy of trade reciprocity assumes that competitors will only negotiate reductions in their trade barriers if they are under the pressure of discriminatory trade measures. The U.S. Export Enhancement Program is an example of such a policy put into practice. The Reagan administration viewed the program as a defensive response to the European Community's "trade-distorting" practices. The United States was prepared to phase out the EEP if the EC would freeze and then eliminate its export subsidies. The program was a partial success. It did increase U.S. political leverage over the EC in GATT trade reform talks. It did not trigger the trade war critics had predicted. Furthermore, the Cairns Group of "fair traders," Canada, Caribbean and Latin American countries, and other non-EC countries perceived it as a justified response to a destabilizing export subsidy program designed to take world grain markets away from the United States. Although the program did not succeed in eliminating the "trade-distorting" practices of EC competitors, it did help restore U.S. dominance of the world grain trade. It also constituted an incentive for the European Community to agree to include export subsidies and even its Common Agricultural Policy on the GATT negotiating agenda—something the community had vowed never to do.

Where a liberal approach to trade policy often fails is in appreciating the significance of political institutions. Runge and Witzke (1987:213) note, for example, that economists tend to accept institutions, such as the EC's Common Agricultural Policy, as a given and therefore do not address the issue of reforming them. Hence liberal analysts have tended to ignore altogether a crucial measure of the success of the Export Enhancement Program: Did it increase the prospects for reforming the CAP? On an answer to this question rests the success or failure of the program's political objective of restoring U.S. dominance of the world grain trade.

Failure to understand the political necessities behind the CAP led the United States to make extreme and unrealistic demands upon the EC during the Uruguay round of the GATT talks: that the Europeans abandon all or most of their farm programs within ten years. The EC is an international institution established by member states and operated strictly according to the terms of the Treaty of Rome. Total food self-sufficiency and national welfare (including economic security for Europe's small-scale farmers) are firmly entrenched principles of that treaty. Any U.S. farm proposal that would, as one of its consequences, force many of Europe's 11 million producers off their farms could only be politically unacceptable to the EC; for it would be tantamount to accepting a farm depression. No government would alow such an outcome.

What success the Export Enhancement Program did have was largely determined by the institutional characteristics of the European Community and its amenability to reform. That is to say, the EEP's success was the product of internal pressures for reforming the Common Agricultural Policy. The principal source of pressure was the perception of inequity and lack of fairness among members of the European Community. The CAP and the financial system of the community have created net transfer effects that are perceived to benefit some members more than others (Runge and Witzke, 1987:218). These transfer effects have engendered political disputes. The United Kingdom has sought to minimize its share of the CAP budget, bringing it into conflict with France, a major beneficiary. Germany has also sought to limit its contributions, while the so-called southern states (including Greece, Spain, and Portugal) have demanded that more of the CAP budget be redirected from the "northern states" toward agricultural development projects in the south. The southern states have also demanded increased protection for their fruits, wine, and olive oil at the expense of commodities produced by the northern states.

The fairness issue has repeatedly arisen because the EC's agricultural budget and annual commodity price support levels must be approved unanimously by the highest political decision-making body of the community, the Council of Ministers representing all twelve member states. It is precisely during periods of low world prices that require agreement on high agricultural support prices that the political conflict within the European Community is most accentuated. The 1986–87 period, when the U.S. Export Enhancement Program was effective was one with just such institutional preconditions. There was a worldwide grain surplus, the world price for wheat was low, and the value of the U.S. dollar was low, all helping to boost the already burdensome cost to the EC of selling its highly subsidized surplus grain exports. Tensions rose within the EC as the British refused to approve budget increases without CAP reform.

But in early 1988, members of the European Community managed to reconcile their disagreements temporarily and agreed to raise the budget ceiling. The reconciliation was undoubtedly prompted by the impending creation of a barrier-free common market in 1993 with 322 million consumers and a combined gross national product of $4.2 trillion. There was just too much at stake to permit a falling out over an agricultural dispute. The increased funding gave the community more financial flexibility to subsidize its farm surpluses; but the added resources proved unnecessary, at least in the short term, because of the dramatic change in the world market situation brought about by the devastating two-year drought in North America. With the U.S. production of cereals reduced and its grain reserves eliminated, the world price of grain went up, reducing the cost of the EC's export subsidies and removing the institutional preconditions necessary for the EEP to exert political pressure on the EC to reduce or eliminate export subsidies.

This change in circumstances neither demonstrates that the Export Enhancement Program was an ineffective political trade weapon nor suggests that a mercantilist policy may not be effective in the future. What it does show is that such a policy must be evaluated primarily in terms of its impact on political institutions. A program like the EEP can only exert political leverage against the EC during heightened member state conflict over sharing the burden of a growing agricultural budget. Once those political tensions are relieved, such a program's political impact is negligible.

For the United States to threaten the EC with the Export Enhancement Program or a similar trade policy (even one with tougher consequences) when the preconditions for such a policy do not exist is misguided. Even when the preconditions are satisfied, a doctrinaire position like the one the United States took during the Uruguay round will most likely lead to failure. A trade policy that threatens others' perceived national interests will only invite political resistance. It will foster internal cohesion in response to external threats.

In contrast, a U.S. trade policy that has the effect of increasing the costs of EC export subsidies will tend to strengthen the hand of member states who oppose an unchecked growth in agricultural expenditures. This shift in political power will increase the political costs within the EC of continuing its policy of subsidizing exports and will indirectly give the United States political leverage. Indeed, 1993 could prove to be the ideal time for the resumption of the EEP or a comparable program. The agricultural policy the EC adopted in 1988 (called the Delors package) had the end of 1991 as its expiration date, forcing the community to negotiate a new agricultural policy once again. The community faces the new financial burden of assisting Eastern European countries and the former Soviet Union. The southern states in the EC, which outnumber the northern states, are still unsatisfied.

It will take more than the EEP or a comparable trade policy, however, to persuade the Europeans to reduce their farm export subsidies. It will be necessary to have a negotiating position that does not threaten their perceived national interests. Doctrinaire positions arguing for total elimination of farm subsidies must be modified. A realistic negotiation position based on some form of market sharing such as the 1987 Harkin Bill would appear to be appropriate. It would empower the president to engage in multilateral negotiations on world market shares. The Export Enhancement Program would provide a backup to ensure that the United States maintains its share of world markets.

Ranking of Companies by Value of EEP Bonuses

Company	Total bonuses[a]	Percentage of total bonuses[b]	Rank
Cargill Inc.	$688,979,570	18.27	1
Continental Grain Co.	$632,990,005	16.79	2
Louis Dreyfus Corp.	$503,742,687	13.36	3
Peavey Co.	$175,966,711	4.67	4
Artfer Inc.	$140,736,584	3.73	5
Pillsbury Co.	$130,324,143	3.46	6
Bunge Corp.	$119,044,556	3.16	7
CAM USA, Inc.	$105,852,126	2.81	8
Garnac Grain Co., Inc.	$105,700,207	2.80	9
Ferruzzi Trading USA, Inc.	$98,891,555	2.62	10
Union Equity Coop. Exchange	$98,351,448	2.61	11
Richco Grain, Ltd.	$95,064,901	2.52	12
J. Aron and Co.	$74,498,514	1.98	13
Alfred C. Toepfer Int'l., Inc.	$71,914,739	1.91	14
Tradigrain, Inc.	$64,967,162	1.72	15
Mitsubishi Int'l.	$49,009,004	1.30	16
ADM Milling Co.	$47,667,207	1.26	17
Gold Kist, Inc.	$46,875,795	1.24	18
Voest-Alpine Trading USA Corp.	$35,607,177	0.94	19
Entrade Int'l., Ltd.	$34,054,788	0.90	20
Coprostates, Inc.	$30,717,697	0.81	21
ConAgra Poultry Co.	$29,109,326	0.77	22
Harvest States Coop.	$28,328,966	0.75	23
Esmah Nevada, Inc.	$21,662,350	0.57	24

Appendix

Company	Total bonuses[a]	Percentage of total bonuses[b]	Rank
Nichimen America, Inc.	$21,504,940	0.57	25
Marubeni America Corp.	$18,745,999	0.50	26
Land O' Lakes, Inc.	$18,380,000	0.49	27
American Marketing Services, Inc.	$17,794,865	0.47	28
Mitsui Grain Corp.	$17,427,849	0.46	29
Bartlett and Co.	$16,684,602	0.44	30
Central States Enterprises, Inc.	$15,936,869	0.42	31
C. Itoh and Co. (America), Inc.	$15,861,999	0.42	32
Carey Agri-Int'l., Inc.	$13,625,850	0.36	33
Tradecom, Inc.	$12,897,349	0.34	34
Int'l. Multifoods	$12,201,518	0.32	35
Alliance Grain, Inc.	$11,551,368	0.31	36
Fast Food Merchandisers, Inc.	$10,460,584	0.28	37
Granplex, Inc.	$9,770,348	0.26	38
Servac Int'l.	$9,729,853	0.26	39
Nissho Iwai American Corp.	$9,556,647	0.25	40
Amber, Inc.	$8,649,001	0.23	41
Froedtert Malt Corp.	$8,223,021	0.22	42
Balfour MacLaine Int'l., Ltd.	$8,148,363	0.22	43
Woodhouse Corp.	$7,536,053	0.20	44
Great Western Malting Co.	$5,808,311	0.15	45
Holstein-Fresian Services, Inc.	$5,612,170	0.15	46
National Food Corp.	$5,428,073	0.14	47
Sunrice, Inc.	$4,744,961	0.13	48
Euro-Maghrib, Inc.	$4,708,562	0.13	49
Italgrani USA, Inc.	$4,391,992	0.12	50
Gress Foods, Inc.	$3,922,524	0.10	51
Luzza Int'l. Livestock Corp.	$3,645,000	0.10	52
Decoster Egg Farms	$3,585,050	0.10	53
Protimex Corp.	$3,533,456	0.09	54
ConAgra Int'l. Fertilizer Co.	$3,348,513	0.09	55
Philipp Brothers, Inc.	$3,161,562	0.08	56
Columbia Grain Int'l., Inc.	$2,034,731	0.05	57
Cereal Food Processors	$1,984,140	0.05	58
CTC North America, Inc.	$1,815,372	0.05	59
Elders Grain, Inc.	$1,607,361	0.04	60
Rahr Malting Co.	$1,592,485	0.04	61
T.K. Int'l., Inc.	$1,490,325	0.04	62
Woodhouse Drake and Carey (Trading)	$1,276,896	0.03	63
Exodus Holsteins	$1,275,720	0.03	64
Dolphin Shipping and Trading	$1,241,028	0.03	65
Interstate Grain Corp.	$1,199,137	0.03	66
American Poultry Int'l., Ltd.	$1,053,545	0.03	67
Brown Swiss Enterprises, Inc.	$1,019,820	0.03	68
Golden Genes, Inc.	$1,014,284	0.03	69

Ranking of Companies by Value of EEP Bonuses

Company	Total bonuses[a]	Percentage of total bonuses[b]	Rank
Fleischmann-Kurth Malting Co.	$622,798	0.02	70
Gulf Pacific Rice Co., Inc.	$599,321	0.02	71
Minnesota Malting Co.	$483,526	0.01	72
First Interstate Trading Co.	$461,679	0.01	73
Incotrade, Inc.	$439,818	0.01	74
Kanematsu USA Inc.	$436,335	0.01	75
Dekker North America, Inc.	$436,000	0.01	76
DSH Livestock Int'l., Inc.	$370,000	0.01	77
Riceland Foods, Inc.	$256,981	0.01	78
Romar Int'l. Georgia, Inc.	$256,353	0.01	79
Hefler and Co.	$245,139	0.01	80
Conagra Int'l., Inc.	$241,462	0.01	81
Supreme Rice Mills, Inc.	$217,280	0.01	82
Wisconsin Holstein Service, Inc.	$185,000	0.01	83
Midwest Livestock Producers	$125,520	0.003	84
Cafcrown Ltd.	$115,984	0.003	85
Hidden Villa Ranch	$96,488	0.003	86
McCall Sanders Marketing	$64,743	0.002	87
World Links, Inc.	$36,120	0.001	88
P.S. Int'l.	$17,820	0.0004	89
United States Egg Marketers	$15,120	0.0004	90
AJC Int'l., Inc.	$4,050	0.0001	91
Milton G. Waldbaum Co.	$2,250	0.0000	92
TOTAL[c]	$3,770,969,104		

Source: Communication from James Warden, Branch Chief, Rules Regulation and Reports Branch, Commodity Credit Corporation, Washington, D.C., September 27, 1991.

[a]Total bonuses awarded based on mean quantities for all commodities.

[b]Exporters' percentage of total mean bonuses awarded.

[c]Discrepancies are due to rounding.

Bibliography

Agnelli, Giovanni. 1989. "The Europe of 1992." *Foreign Affairs* 68.

Anthan, George. 1988. "Cargill Joins Consumer Groups against Export Subsidies." *Cargill Bulletin*, October.

Australian Bureau of Agricultural and Resource Economics. 1985. *Agricultural Policies in the European Community*. Policy Monograph 1. Canberra: Australian Government Publishing Service.

——. 1986. *Agricultural Policies in the European Economy*. Policy Monograph 2. Canberra: Australian Government Publishing Service.

——. 1989a. *The 1988 EC Budget and Production Stabilizers*. Discussion Paper 89.3. Canberra: Australian Government Publishing Service.

——. 1989b. *U.S. Grain Policies and the World Market*. Policy Monograph 4. Canberra: Australian Government Publishing Service.

Barkema, Alan, and Mark Drabenstott. 1988. "Can U.S. and Great Plains Agriculture Compete in the World Market?" *Economic Review* (Federal Reserve Bank of Kansas City), February.

Bhagwati, Jagdish N., and Douglas A. Irwin. 1987. "The Return to the Reciprocitarians: U.S. Trade Policy." *World Economy* 10.

Borrus, Michael; Laura D'Andrea Tyson; and John Zysman. 1986. "Creating Advantage: How Government Policies Shape International Trade in the Semiconductor Industry." In *Strategic Trade Policy and the New International Economy*, ed. Paul R. Krugman. Cambridge: MIT Press.

Cathie, John. 1985. "U.S. and EEC Agricultural Trade Policies: A Long-Run View of the Present Conflict." *Food Policy* 10.

Cline, William R. 1982. *Reciprocity: A New Approach to World Trade Policy?* Policy Analyses in International Economics 3. Washington, D.C.: Institute for International Economics.

Commission of the European Communities. 1986. *The European Community Budget: The Facts.* Brussels: CEC.

———. 1988. *The Agricultural Situation in the Community: 1987 Report.* Brussels: CEC.

———. 1991. *The Agricultural Situation in the Community: 1990 Report.* Brussels: CEC.

Congressional Quarterly. 1984. *Farm Policy: The Politics of Soil Surpluses and Subsidies.* Washington, D.C.: Congressional Quarterly.

Cresson, Edith. 1985. "French Attitude to a New GATT Round." *World Economy* 8.

Crowder, Richard T. 1989. Statement by under secretary for International Affairs and Commodity Programs, U.S. Department of Agriculture, before the Subcommittee on Wheat, Soybeans, and Feed Grains, House Committee on Agriculture, 101st Congr., 1st sess., July 31.

Curzon, Gerard, and Victoria Curzon. 1976. *The Multilateral Trading System of the 1960s.* Vol. 1, *International Economic Relations of the Western World.* London: Oxford University Press.

Dam, Kenneth W. 1970. *The GATT: Law and International Economic Organization.* Chicago: University of Chicago Press.

Dell, Edmund. 1984. "Trade Policy: Retrospect and Prospect." *International Affairs* 60.

———. 1986. "Of Free Trade and Reciprocity." *World Economy* 9.

———. 1987. *The Politics of Economic Interdependence.* New York: St. Martin's.

Dunmore, John C. 1986. "Competitiveness and Comparative Advantage of U.S. and Southern Agriculture." ERS/USDA paper presented at the Conference on Competitiveness of Southern Agriculture, Atlanta, November 4–6.

Engles, Wolfram, et al. 1985. "The CAP Is Destroying the EEC." *Economic Affairs* 5.

European Community Information Service. 1959. *Second General Report on the Activities of the Community.* March 31.

Friend, Reed E. 1985. "Agricultural Outlook." Washington, D.C.: U.S. Department of Agriculture.

General Agreement on Tariffs and Trade. 1969. *Basic Instruments and Selected Documents* (BISD), Vol. 4 (March). Geneva: Contracting Parties to the GATT.

———. 1985. *Agreement on Trade in Civil Aircraft.* Geneva: GATT.

[141]

Bibliography

Gilpin, Robert. 1975. *U.S. Power and the Multinational Corporation: The Political Economy of Foreign Direct Investment.* New York: Basic Books.

——. 1987. *The Political Economy of International Relations.* Princeton: Princeton University Press.

Goldstein, Judith, and Stephen D. Krasner. 1984. "Unfair Trade Practices: The Case for a Differential Response." *American Economic Review* 74.

Harvey, David R. 1986. "The CAP, International Policies and the Changing Outlook for Cereals." Paper to ARS/SFER Seminar, Wye College, September.

Hathaway, Dale E. 1987. *Agriculture and the GATT: Rewriting the Rules.* Washington, D.C.: Institute for International Economics.

Higgott, Richard A., and Andrew Fenton Cooper. 1990. "Middle Power Leadership and Coalition Building: Australia, the Cairns Group, and the Uruguay Round of Trade Negotiations." *International Organization* 44.

Hillman, Jimmye S. 1978. *Nontariff Agricultural Trade Barriers.* Lincoln: University of Nebraska Press.

Hindley, Brian, and Alasdair MacBean. 1986. "Edmund Dell's Manifesto for Mercantilist Liberation." *World Economy* 9.

Huhne, Christopher. 1985. *The Forces Shaping British Attitudes towards the EC.* London: Centre for European Policy Studies.

Johnson, D. Gale. 1950. *Trade and Agriculture: A Study of Inconsistent Policies.* New York: Wiley.

Jones, Daniel T. 1980. "British Industrial Regeneration: The European Dimension." In *Budgetary Politics: The Finance of the European Communities,* ed. Helen Wallace. London: Allen & Unwin.

Kindleberger, Charles P. 1978. *Economic Response: Comparative Studies in Trade, Finance, and Growth.* Cambridge: Harvard University Press.

Krasner, Steven. D. 1983. *International Regimes.* Ithaca, N.Y.: Cornell University Press.

——. 1985. *Structural Conflict: The Third World against Global Liberalism.* Berkeley and Los Angeles: University of California Press.

Krugman, Paul R. 1979. "Increasing Returns, Monopolistic Competition, and International Trade." *Journal of International Economics* 9.

——. 1983. "New Theories of Trade among Industrial Countries." *American Economic Review: Papers and Proceedings of the 95th Annual Meetings of the American Economic Association* 73 (May).

——, ed. 1986. *Strategic Trade Policy and the New International Economics.* Cambridge: MIT Press.

———. 1987. "Is Free Trade Passé?" *Economic Perspectives* 1.

Lipson, Charles. 1982. "The Transformation of Trade: The Sources and Effects of Regime Change." *International Organization* 36.

Lipton, Michael. 1987. Forward to Paul Streeten, *What Price Food?: Agricultural Price Policies in Developing Countries*. Ithaca, N.Y.: Cornell University Press.

McCoy, Steven A. 1989. Statement by the president of the North American Export Grain Association before the House Subcommittee on Wheat, Soybeans, and Feed Grains. 101st Congr., 1st sess., April 27.

Morgan, Ann D. 1980. "The Balance of Payments and British Membership of the European Community." In *Budgetary Politics: The Finance of the European Communities,* ed. Helen Wallace. London: Allen & Unwin.

Morgan, Dan. 1980. *Merchants of Grain*. New York: Penguin.

Organisation for Economic Co-operation and Development. 1987. *National Politics and Agricultural Trade: United States*. Paris: OECD.

Paarlberg, Don. 1984. *Purposes of Farm Policy*. AEI Occasional Papers. Washington, D.C.: American Enterprise Institute for Public Policy Research.

Paarlberg, Robert L. 1988. *Fixing Farm Trade: Policy Options for the United States*. Cambridge: Ballinger.

———. 1989. "A Closer Look at EEP." Remarks at Congressional Research Seminar on agricultural export programs, Washington, D.C., November 20.

Patrick, Stephanie. 1985. "Administration Agrees to Export Subsidies in Exchange for Support on Budget Cuts." *Cargill Bulletin,* June.

Pearson, Charles, and Nils Johnson. 1986. *The New GATT Trade Round*. Washington, D.C.: School of Advanced International Studies, Johns Hopkins University.

Rapp, David. 1988. *How the U.S. Got into Agriculture and Why It Can't Get Out*. Washington, D.C.: Congressional Quarterly.

Rosecrance, Richard. 1985. *The Rise of the Trading State*. New York: Basic Books.

Ruggie, John Gerard. 1982. "International Regimes, Transactions, and Change: Embedded Liberalism in the Postwar Economic Order." *International Organization* 36.

Rugman, Alan M. 1986. "U.S. Protectionism and the Canadian Trade Policy." *Journal of World Trade Law* 20.

Rugman, Alan M., and Andrew D. M. Anderson. 1987. *Administered Protection in America*. London: Croom Helm.

Runge, C. Ford. 1989. "Reforming Agricultural Policy: The Irrelevance of 'Free Trade.'" Manuscript.

Runge, C. Ford, and Harald von Witzke. 1987. "Institutional Change in the Common Agricultural Policy of the European Community." *American Journal of Agricultural Economics* 69.

Schaeffer, Jon. 1989. "New USTR Promises to Get Tough on Unfair Trade." News release issued by American Embassy in New Zealand. January 27.

Schuh, G. E. 1984. "United States Agriculture in the World Economy." *Journal of Agribusiness* 2.

Schuh, G. E., and H. Cleveland. 1986. "North American Grain Production in World Affairs." In *The Future of the North American Granary: Politics, Economics and Resource Constraints in North American Agriculture*, ed. C. Ford Runge. Ames: Iowa State University Press.

Shape, Richard H. 1988. "Is Non-Discrimination Really Dead?" *World Economy* 11.

Smith, Adam. 1947. *The Wealth of Nations*. London: Dent "Everyman."

Spence, A. Michael. 1984. "Industrial Organization and Competitive Advantage in Multinational Industry." *American Economic Review* 74.

Strange, Marty, et al. 1989. *The Great Trade Debate*. Walthill, Neb.: Center for Rural Affairs.

Strange, Susan. 1985. "Protectionism and World Politics." *International Organization* 39.

Tangerman, S. 1985. "Special Features and Ongoing Reforms of the CAP." In *Confrontation or Negotiation: United States Policy and European Agriculture*, ed. C. E. Curry, W. P. Nichols, and R. P. Purnell. Millwood, N.Y.: Associated Faculty Press.

Taylor, Paul. 1982. "The EC Crisis over the Budget and the Agricultural Policy: Britain and Its Partners in the Late 1970s and Early 1980s." *Government and Opposition* 17.

Tracy, Michael. 1982. *Agriculture in Western Europe: Challenge and Response, 1880–1980*. London: Granada.

U.S. Department of Agriculture. 1987. "FAS Fact Sheet: Export Enhancement Program." Washington, D.C.: USDA.

———. 1989. *World Grain Situation and Outlook*. Foreign Agricultural Service FG 4-89. Washington, D.C.: USDA.

———. 1990. "Profiles of Agriculture in the United States and European Community." In *Western Europe Agriculture and Trade Report*, co-ord. Walter H. Gardiner and Mary Lisa Madell. Economic Research Service RS-90-4. Washington, D.C.: USDA.

U.S. General Accounting Office. 1989. "Status Report on GAO's Review of the Export Enhancement Program." Statement of Allan I. Mendelowitz, director Trade, Energy and Finance Issues, National Security and International Affairs Division before the Subcommittee on Wheat, Soybeans and Feed Grains, Committee on Agriculture, House of Representatives. 101st Congr., 1st sess., July 31.

——. 1990. *International Trade: Activity under the Export Enhancement Program.* GAO/NSLAD-90-59FS. Washington, D.C.: GAO.

U.S. House of Representatives. 1987. *Trade and International Economy Policy Reform Act of 1987.* 100th Congr., 1st sess., April 6. Rept. 100-40, pt. 3.

——. Committee on Agriculture. 1985. *Review of the Export Enhancement Program Announced by the U.S. Department of Agriculture.* Hearings before the Subcommittee on Department Operations, Research, and Foreign Agriculture. 99th Congr., 1st sess., October 8, 10, and November 5. Serial 9916.

——. Committee on Appropriations. Subcommittee on Rural Development, Agriculture, and Related Agencies. 1988. *Rural Development, Agriculture and Related Agencies Appropriations for 1989: Excerpts from Hearings.* Pt. 4. 100th Congr., 2d sess., March 9.

U.S. National Commission on Agricultural Trade and Export Policy. 1986. *Executive Summary of the Report to the President and Congress of the United States of America: Concluding Recommendations.* Washington, D.C.: Government Printing Office.

Viner, Jacob. 1969. "Power versus Plenty as Objectives of Foreign Policy in the Seventeenth and Eighteenth Centuries." In *Revisions in Mercantilism,* ed. D. C. Coleman. London: Meuthuen.

Warley, T. K. 1976. "Agricultural Protectionism and Trade Policies." In *International Economic Relations of the Western World, 1959–1971,* ed. Andrew Shonfield. London: Oxford University Press.

Wessel, James. 1983. *Trading the Future.* San Francisco: Institute for Food and Development Policy.

Yao-Su Hu. 1979. "German Agricultural Power: The Impact on France and Britain." *World Today,* November.

Yoffie, David B. 1986. "Strategy, Structure and American Trade Policy." Working paper, Harvard Business School, 9-786-028.

Yoon, Young-Kwan. 1987. "The Irony of Plenty: Japanese Foreign Direct Investment and Productivity." Paper presented at the 1987 Annual Meeting of the American Political Science Association, Chicago.

Index

Index

[148]

Index

political costs of EEP, 10, 85, 86–
89, 115–17, 128–30
refusal to negotiate CAP, 124, 129–
30
rejection of U.S. GATT proposal,
119–20
shift in political power, 111–12
Single European Act, 2–3, 112,
133–34
Spanish accession, 111, 128n
Treaty of Rome, 102n
unfair trade practices, 13
and the United States, 4–5, 47, 49,
69–85
U.S. pressure to negotiate reductions in subsidies, 1, 128–30
Export Enhancement Program (EEP),
1
arguments for, 8–10
bargaining chip in Uruguay round,
59, 115–30
barley export subsidies, 74–77
bonuses, 73–76
commodities, 54
competition with EC subsidies, 11,
23, 25, 53–58, 69–77
Congress and administration conflict, 57–66
controversy over targeting markets,
61–63
countries excluded, 61
criteria for EEP sales, 59
criticism of, 6–8, 10, 12, 59–60,
65, 69–71
evaluation of, 10, 77–85
exclusion of USSR, 61–63
expansion of U.S. markets, 60, 77–
78
export sales, 53–55, 57, 81
financial authorization, 58–59, 130
first initiatives, 55, 68–70
increasing conflict in EC, 26, 81–
85, 115–17, 131–32
interagency government review
system, 55–57
liberal trade theory, 12, 132
markets in China, 53, 55, 78
markets in USSR, 53–55, 78
North African markets, 53, 61, 78

objectives, 52–66, 77
operation, 53–57, 63–66
potential to reform EC, 133–35
preconditions for success, 132–35
pressure on the EC, 53, 81–85,
115–17
Reagan administration and, 49,
58–59, 115–16, 119, 122–23,
131
restoration of U.S. markets, 77–81
"second best" gain in trade, 23
stimulation of U.S. exports, 77
strategic trade policy, 17
surplus disposal program, 12, 59
trade-distoring practices, 131
U.S. companies and, 55, 137–39
U.S. foreign policy and, 86
wheat export subsidies, 71–74

Fair traders. See Cairns Group
Farm prices
British-French compromise on, 97
British opposition to increases, 89,
90, 92–94
German opposition to cuts, 100–
101
France
agrifood credit, 67–68
alienation of the farm vote, 103
Chinese grain markets, 80–81
cohabitation, 103
commitment to CAP, 44, 86–87
comparative advantage, 105
competition for grain markets, 69–
77
dominated markets, 61
EC agricultural policy, 87–88
EC budget, 86–87
export strategy, 67–69
farmer protests, 90, 92
farm price increases, 96, 98–99,
103–5
French farmers' union, 103
grain exports, 31–35, 67–69, 80–
81
grain production, 31–35, 67–69,
114
grain storage subsidies, 43
markets under U.S. pressure, 68–
77

[149]

Index

France (*cont.*)
net gain from EAGGF, 40–43
North African markets, 80–81
opposition to British policy, 43–
46, 86–87, 94–95
Rally for the Republic, 97
refusal to negotiate subsidies, 120
socialist doctrine, 87–89
Soviet grain markets, 67–69, 80–
81
U.S. demands, 105
French National Cereals Office
(ONIC), 80
Friend, Reed, 34
Fritz, Richard, 63–64

General Agreement on Tariffs and
Trade (GATT), 3–5
agricultural exemption, 118
Bush administration policy, 65–66
civil aircraft, 25
EC concessions to United States,
127–28, 131
EEP as trade weapon, 1, 26, 59,
115–17, 130, 134–35
equitable share of trade, 118
export subsidies, 118
fifteen-point program, 3
initial breakdown, 4–5
inter-American support for United
States, 123–24
Kennedy round, 4
market-sharing proposal, 127
ministerial declaration by Switzerland and Colombia, 121
Montreal conference of 1988, 129
most favored nation, 21
negotiations stall, 128–30
original treaty, 118
Reagan administration proposals,
3, 65, 115–16, 119–20, 125
Tokyo round, 4
Uruguay round, 2–5, 65, 119–20,
124–30
U.S. conditions for participation,
119
U.S. farm policy, 118n
Germany
alliance with Britain, 101
alliance with France, 10

cereal price increases, 100–101,
103–4, 106–7
Christian Democratic Union, 104
Christian Social Union, 104
contributions to EAGGF, 41–43
electoral threat, 100–101, 104
Free Democratic Party, 87
Social Democratic Party, 101, 104
trade surplus, 25
U.S. trading relationship with, 19,
25
Goldstein, Judith, 22
Green currencies. See Monetary com-
pensatory amounts
Guerrilla trade warfare, 49
Guillaume, François, 92, 103–4

Harkin Bill of 1987, 135
Harvey, David, 8–9
Hathaway, Dale, 33, 49, 66
Hawke, Bob, 122–23
Higgott, Richard A., 122
Hills, Carla, 5, 65–66
Home Grown Cereals Authority, 72–
76
Howe, Sir Geoffrey, 91
Huhne, Christopher, 43

International costs of production,
15n
International Dairy Agreement, 49,
125
International Wheat Council, 112
Irwin, Douglas A., 21

Japan, 13, 19
Jopling, Michael, 99, 100

Kay, Thomas, 77–78, 126
Kerin, John, 123
Kiechle, Ignaz, 97, 100–101, 104, 106
Kohl, Helmut, 101
Krasner, Stephen, 22
Krugman, Paul, 17

Leahy, Patrick, 129–30
Louis Dreyfus Corporation, 57
Lyng, Richard, 128

McCoy, Steven, 26
McGuire, Dan, 58, 60

[150]

McPherson, Peter, 3
Major trading blocs, 2–3
Mansholt, Sicco, 36
Mauroy, Pierre, 96–97
Mercantilist trade policies, 1, 18–19
    aggressive retaliation, 22, 133–35
    counterproductive potential, 134
    defined, 17–20
    German trade policy, 19
    Hobbesian state of nature, 18
    institution preconditions, 132–33
    national economic interests, 18–22
    objectives, 18–20
    reciprocity, 20–22
Mitterrand, François, 87, 95, 97, 103, 120
Monetary compensatory amounts (MCAs), 42–43, 90, 98, 105
Morgan, Ann D., 44

National interest, 12, 14, 49, 134
NATO, 49
Noir, Michel, 105
Nonsubsidizing wheat exporters. See Cairns Group
North American Export Grain Association, 26
Norway, 60

Paarlberg, Don, 12
Paarlberg, Robert, 6–8, 10
Plumb, Sir Henry, 94
Pompidou, Georges, 103
Portugal, 111

Reagan administration, 3
    budget resolution of 1985, 58–59
    opposition to EEP, 59
    proposals to GATT, 3, 65, 115–16, 119–20, 125
    trade retaliation, 105, 115–16
Reciprocal Trade Agreements Act of 1934, 20–21
Roberts, Ivan, 17, 51–52, 82–83
Rocard, Michel, 88, 98–99
Rosecrance, Richard, 19
Runge, C. Ford, 132

Schmidt, Helmut, 87, 90
Schuh, G. E., 22–23
Secrétariat Général du Comité Inter-

ministériel pour les Questions Européennes (SGCI), 40
Smith, Adam, 18–19
Stoltenberg, Gerhardt, 100
Strange, Marty, 14
Strange, Susan, 24
Strategic trade policy, 17

Tangerman, S., 12
Taylor, Paul, 44
Thatcher, Margaret
    conflict with Chirac, 109–10
    grievances toward CAP, 45–46, 86–87
    reform of CAP, 103
Trade theory. See Mercantilist trade policies; United States: doctrinaire trade theory
Tugendhat, Christopher, 91

United Kingdom
    CAP as scapegoat, 44–45
    dispute with France, 86–92
    EC budget refund, 88–89
    economic decline, 45
    grievances toward CAP, 43–46, 100–101
    members of European Parliament, 94, 96
    National Farmers' Union, 94
    Navigation Acts of Parliament, 18
    opposition to CAP, 45–46
    opposition to farm price increases, 89, 90–92
    trade deficit, 44
    veto of Delors plan, 108
United States
    balance of payments, 1
    decline in dollar, 13, 51, 63, 126–27, 133
    doctrinaire trade theory, 125, 132, 134–35
    and the European Community, 4–5, 47, 49, 69–85
    Gulf price of wheat, 70n
    Harkin Bill of 1987, 135
United States–Canada Free Trade Agreement, 2
United States–Mexico trade agreement, 2

[151]

Index

Library of Congress Cataloging-in-Publication Data

Libby, Ronald T.
  Protecting markets : U.S. policy and the world grain trade / Ronald T. Libby.
    p. cm.
  Includes bibliographical references (p.) and index.
  ISBN 0-8014-2617-0 (alk. paper)
  1. Grain trade—Government policy—United States. I. Title.
HD9036.L53   1992
382'.4131'0973—dc20   91-55536